EARTH AND SECOND EARTH

The Collected Works of Gregge Tiffen

P Systems & Associates, Publishers
La Jolla, California

Copyright 2010
By
G-Systems International

All Rights Reserved

———————

ISBN: 978-0-9842552-8-3

P Systems & Associates, Publishers
La Jolla, California

Earth and Second Earth
Published by P Systems & Associates
P.O. Box 12754
La Jolla, CA 92039
www.P-SystemsInc.com

While we appreciate your enthusiasm for sharing our work, please remind yourself of what you know about copyrighted information. Here's a refresher: All rights Reserved. No parts of this publication may be reproduced, stored in or introduced into a retrieval system, or transmitted, in any form or by any means (electronic, mechanical, photocopying, recording or otherwise), without the prior written consent. The scanning, uploading, and distribution of this book via the Internet or by any other means without the permission of G-Systems International is illegal and punishable by law. Your support of these rights is appreciated. Thank you.

To contact G-Systems International, visit www.g-systems.com, email Bonnie@g-systems.com, or call 1-972-447-9092.

For general information about other publications, visit our web site www.P-SystemsInc.com or call our toll free number 1.888.658.0668.

Transcribed and written by Patrece Powers
Graphic Designer: Isla Cordelae
Editorial assistance: Cindy Reinhardt
                      Isla Cordelae
                      Renne Evans

Printed in the United States of America
on 80% post consumer recycled paper

We offer deep appreciation to the astral volunteers whose experience, knowledge, and dedication consistently benefits us in all the seen and unseen ways.

These Works of mysticism update that which would otherwise be left behind.

--Gregge Tiffen

Contents

Introduction: The Collected Works. 1

Heaven on Earth 3
  1. Motivation. 3
  2. Protection 4
  3. Etheric Administration 4
  4. Inter-Level Communication 5
  5. Communication Procedure. 6
  6. Astral Volunteers 7
  7. On Assignment. 10
  8. Etheric Participants 11
  9. Levels in the Hierarchy 13
  10. Reincarnation Board Considerations 14
  11. Types of Incarnations. 15
  12. The Council Level 16
  13. The Master Level 16
  14. The Avatar Grouping 17
  15. The Avatar Concept 18
  16. Mythology 18
  17. The Divinity of Man 20
  18. Spiritual Mathematics 23
  19. The Unity of Creation 25
  20. The Law of Action 32
  21. Seeking 33
  22. Finding 34
  23. Messengers 35

Beyond Telepathy 37
  1. Telepathy 37
  2. Telemetry 38
  3. Psychotelemetry 39
  4. Comparisons. 39
  5. Basic Premise in Mysticism. 41
  6. Parabolic 42
  7. Techniques in Selection 43

    8. Spiritual Terminal. 45
    9. Mental Terminal 46
  10. Physical Terminal 46
  11. Activator Terminal 47
  12. Targets 48
  13. The Atom. 49
  14. Gathering Information 50
  15. Consistent Resistance Factors 51
  16. Beyond Telepathy 52

The Power of Observation 53
    1. Individualized Thought 54
    2. Concentrated Energy 55
    3. The Universal Flow 56
    4. Harmonious Interaction 57
    5. Transmission 59
    6. Changing Frequencies 59
    7. New Aspects of Thought 60

The Ubiquitous Soul 63
    1. Divine Action 65
    2. Separation 65
    3. Individuality 67
    4. Dependency 68
    5. Duality 69
    6. Unity 71
    7. The Soul Memory Drum 73
    8. Soul Mate Theory De-Bugged 76
    9. Similar Experiences 77
  10. Energy Impress 78
  11. Illuminated 81
  12. Energy Points 82
  13. Singular Unity 83
  14. The Ubiquitous Soul 85

Conclusion: To Earth from Second Earth. 87

Introduction
The Collected Works

The Collected Works is a compilation of presentations from Gregge Tiffen's lectures and teachings to which the reader can return beneficially time and time again. Gregge had little time to write due to the sheer magnitude of teaching and lecturing activities that increased year-by-year throughout more than five decades of his work in the field of meta-energy. In addition to his business consultations and lectures, his days were spent meeting the needs of people who sought guidance for personal and professional concerns.

He consistently refused requests to form an organization of any kind in order to insure that his unique training in mysticism, including the Universal Laws of Independence and Individuality, would find the proper audience. He felt certain that such teachings must not be frame-worked within organizations. By their very design, organizations develop a hierarchy of personalities that regrettably destroy the atmosphere necessary for the purity required to learn and to teach, to lead and to follow.

The style and presentation of materials published in this series of The Collected Works are Gregge's unaltered spoken words. There is very little editorial license in order to maintain the clarity of precision that identifies how he was taught and, as a result, how he taught. The timeless nature of knowledge precludes indicating dates and locations of his teachings. In this way, we are able to support and promote the integrity of Gregge's life-long dedication to up-date and correct misinterpretations of ancient wisdoms.

2 Earth and Second Earth

Since all lectures were delivered to an audience familiar with Gregge's mystical training and orientation, we suggest those who are unacquainted with those principles familiarize themselves by reading his highly acclaimed book: *Life in the World Hereafter, The Journey Continues.* It is truly an adventure you won't want to miss. Don't leave earth without it!

Part I
Heaven on Earth

> *There is no greater love than the empathy*
> *we have from our etheric helpers.*
> *Doing something with it is up to us.*
> *--GT*

Beginning in the early 1980's, a major galaxial change occurred when the galaxy made a right hand turn. Planet Earth is positioned at the end of our galaxy, and we experience the turn as a whiplash effect. In fact, there is a transitional period occurring until 2030 due to this huge vortexual change. It's immaterial if you don't want change, or if you don't want to understand it. This transitional change says, "You better move along or I am going to run right over you."

In order not to be entrapped in the commonality of the fear of change, you rise above it into the reality that your power cannot be taken away. Power and responsibility are best exercised with the understanding that there is not any system that has dictatorial control over your life. You always have the power of choice and application wherever you find yourself in the Universe. Courage is the directive in your life. To recognize that as a reality (and to live by it) comes from you understanding that the power to accept or to resist is individual choice.

Motivation

Motivation for identity, individuality, and power is a responsibility. You have the knowledge, as a means of protection, to apply this power with very definite support. That support is a communication procedure set up for you to communicate between the incarnate and discarnate levels. In other words, there is support for you as it pertains to the inter-levels of communication between the seen and the unseen activities of existence. This brings us to the consideration of the visible and non-visible energies operating as if knitted together in one unit while operating independently.

Protection

Knowledge is a means of protection. There is very definite support from the non-physical as a means to access knowledge. Let me remind you that your assignment on planet earth is a post-graduate type activity. You have the trilogy of the spiritual, mental, and physical frequencies operating through the one vehicle we call a body. However, it would defeat the means and methodology of what this curriculum is all about if you were to consider such a system as a deal-making supplication to heaven, to the Universe, or (if you prefer) to some kind of God. That would be a limitation. Yes, heaven is responding, but the communication procedure that is being used by the masses is not accurate. If it were, it would be far more effective than it is.

Etheric Administration

There are levels in the etheric realms, just as there are levels in our society. You can be assured that in an omnipotent, all-powerful Universe there *are* major administrative areas within the whole planetary school system. In fact, every planet, in every solar system, and in every galaxy has a hierarchy as part of the universal structure. In other words, this hierarchical structure I am going to talk about operates on every planet, in every solar system, and in every galaxy throughout the Universe.

There is a hierarchy with an efficient methodology. The power of the hierarchy's main job is over-all administration for both the incarnate and discarnate areas. *They* are aware of all the positive and negative conditions that have to be acted upon here and there. However, awareness of an individual is not their job except as the individual is a part of the whole. T*hey* are very, very busy in *their* administrative work. Nevertheless, if there is a massive concern, such as a war or an earthquake, *they* are aware of the nature of it and the probable effect.

The *Powers-that-Be* have their hands full to make sure that what is meant to be a positive experience is not overwhelmed by the very negative plane that exists in the discarnate area. The input of negativity, by way of the discarnate plane, is fed to us in our incarnate state, and the negativity from us in the incarnate is fed to the discarnate state. The discarnate negative plane is very hard to deal with and is extremely dangerous, but the hierarchical structure is set up in such a way that there are administrators for all areas of responsibility.

Inter-Level Communication

Who is listening during a communication with the discarnates? *Everyone* is listening but not everyone is going to act because that would be a violation on *their* part. An example of that level of inter-communicative responsibility is like going from the mayor of a city, to the governor, to the senator, to the President of the United States. You are just not going to call on the President for something that the mayor can handle, but the mayor will pass your message along to the President if it is appropriate. We are talking about a vast area and a lot of problems that are being addressed by the etheric hierarchy administration.

Communication Procedure

To have direct communication with the hierarchy administrators would make you the target of a frequency input that far exceeds your ability to receive such intensity. Even an attempt to communicate directly with you from the administrative level would blow out your circuitry. Therefore, the energy is toned down through other channels for you. In other words, messages are passed along indirectly, not directly. Nevertheless, such input from higher levels is done and it is done often. *They* want to get the news out and through to you, so *they* use lower channels. The Source of the message is 'X' and the message is received through 'Y'.

It is a load on the astral level when there is a war down here and a large wave of individuals arrive on the other side. The message from the astral realm is something like this, *Look. Here is what is going on. We can use your help. Stand on your own two feet and contribute in a positive way.* That is why it is important for us to know how the communication procedure is designed. Of course there are segments of great beauty in small areas of the astral. However, right now we are talking about the difficult and the confusing, and how our negativity feeds into it. That is why it is important for us to recognize that there is a highly technical procedure in place. That technical procedure is necessary to keep the planet traveling correctly on its galaxial pathway in its vortex.

This sends us back to look at ourselves because all of

this means that you accept a great deal of your own responsibility. Within you resides the ability to realize that there is a high range of activity going on all the time. You *do* know that you are an integral part of the Universe and Its communication procedure.

Astral Volunteers

Primarily for this difficult school, the first level of astral entities between you (in the incarnate) and the discarnate area is a group of volunteers who provide a direct line between you and the Hierarchy. These volunteers are assigned to you on an individual basis. None, at this particular level, have ever been related to you as previous family members. Each of them exceeds your experience by at least fifty percent in their karmic experience, in their states of consciousness, and in their creativity. They are harmonic to you, and the more you expand upon what you do, the more these entities have to do.

I often refer to these groups of advisors as a *Band of Associates*. All metaphysical support comes directly to you from this advisory group of volunteers. Each of these technical advisors is available to you seven days a week, twenty-four hours a day, with no sleep, and with no time off for holidays. They are fully available to you nine months before birth, during your mother's pregnancy, and until your last breath in this incarnation. Their availability is predicated upon your initial pattern when you incarnated. You met them very briefly just before you were assigned to return, but the meeting was not a big ceremony. *Here is your pattern. Here are your people who are absolutely the right kind of people for you. Go for it!* The idea for the meeting is to get your communication procedure intensely established with your *Band of Associates* as your advisors.

As the saying goes, *God helps those who help themselves*. Just because other people are moaning and groaning and want you to moan and groan with them does not mean you should ignore your birthright (your own identification) with your *Band of Associates*. However, just because *they* are there does not mean *they* do anything for you. They are there to assist and instruct you and to pass information to you. These entities get through to you with an energy impress that you feel as inner guidance when you are willing to be aware. Together, you proceed into each event which is the unity. It does not undermine your own power when you move the attention of your thought to your *Band of Associates*. That is the way you generate and update knowledge for advancement of yourself and for humanity. Why would you turn off that access and not use that connection?

You do not need to know any details such as their names, colors, or whatever else might occur to you from Hollywood theatrics. *They* are listening, *they* can transmit to you, and *they* can transmit 'up the line' if what you have to say is needed 'up the line'. What you might call transcendental awareness is something that is transmitted up the line from your *Band* whenever necessary. It isn't who you are communicating with but rather why you are communicating in the first place. Once you recognize *they* are there, what is it you are going to say? Are you registering a complaint? Are you making a request? Is this communication necessary, or can you take care of this yourself? Are you looking for information value when you are communicating at a higher level?

Your awareness is equal to the Source from which it comes. *They* are more aware of the situation than you are, so what you do is talk about clarification of direction that you want in order to progress under the current circumstances. It is bad manners to give half of your attention and to talk to *them* when you are in the midst of doing something else.

Asking for answers you don't want is also impolite. Neither is it the time for communication when you are upset, angry, or fearful. When you have the time and the place, give your full attention to the communication. Realize that you only deal with one aspect of your life at a time. They are dealing with the whole aspect of your life. They are committed to your welfare. I think that deserves a *thank you* for having their finger in the pot at all times, don't you? Let them know you know *they* are there by keeping the line open. Not to listen is such a waste. Why go and talk to people who are not listening and who are not interested?

You have a grandstand seat on evolvement for an intelligent experience with an opportunity that no one else can have. It is your seat, and when you put yourself in alignment with this spiritual system, it works every time. When you focus more and more on the Universe, the answer flashes upon you. It is your *Band of Associates* that knows what you are looking for. *Their* training is to learn how to transmit to you and where *they* can transmit in order to connect with you.

We all go through the same kind of communication procedure in the incarnate state. When someone is a great teacher, it is the same thread. The difference between the teachers and those around them is that the teachers know what they have to do to communicate, how the procedure works, and how they are going to use what they receive. They know what is going to be there all of the time and they use it. You can recognize a teacher by sincerity. Truth, success, and spiritual awareness need no trumpets or drums. It is the vibratory rate that increases and this occurs with consistency and sincerity.

On Assignment

All people who incarnate are sent here (and willingly agree) to do a job that is dependent upon training, development, and lifestyle considerations. Ego warping weaknesses occur when people set up any kind of yardstick of comparison. That is the worst thing anyone can do. So, what is it going to take for you to administer your job? Applaud your *Band of Associates*. Enjoy working with this system consistently because consistency establishes a vortex, and that is your responsibility to yourself. Take the information in, and distill it into your own knowledgeable terms because it is your essence that makes the system work for you. You then become strong in your conviction of who you are and what you are doing. No matter what the world says, you stick to it.

The Life Force is all one and the same on the incarnate and the discarnate levels. Whatever is happening here has a parallel in the discarnate, and there is no deadwood. On an individual level, you are operating as a total unit taking on responsibility but that is the joy of expressing, expanding, and creating. That is not burdensome! You are not alone in terms of administration, but you *are* responsible to learn as quickly as possible to take on more energy usage. You are independent, but you are never ever isolated anywhere in the Universe. There is always another consciousness whose realm of awareness incorporates your need. That is the responsibility of the hierarchy. There is a quality and a level of intelligence that is efficient to meet the magnitude and volume of consciousness necessary to meet all conditions.

The Universe is doing what it is supposed to be doing, and how you do what you do determines the quality of each event. Sustaining a mass of energy in order to bring it into manifestation is the doing. What we are considering here is the amount of energy expended and the ability to maintain it. You *feel* the action, and you feel you in it. That feeling provides the movement and vibration in order to have an experience, and the experience then provides you with a reference point. Yes, the empathy and rapport with the astral is fantastic, but the work is yours to do.

Etheric Participants

Your consciousness travels from galaxy to galaxy within an infinite amount of galaxies throughout the Universe. That is the process of gathering knowledge through experience. It is the action that creates the opportunity for experience. In its travels to the galaxy of choice, consciousness chooses to go to only one solar system within that galaxy. It is the solar system that is its secondary goal. Then, the planet within the solar system provides the level of execution for whatever energy may be required for consciousness in the knowledge gathering experience. Consciousness can and will assume some form of energy as an energy vortex, but that is not necessarily a physical form as it is on our planet.

1. The Asher - Your Personal Protector

The polarity to this planet is the astral realm. Your consciousness, as an energy vortex, is currently contained in a physical vehicle that we call a body. You have a personal protector surrounding you at all times in the form of energy. We call this energy an Asher. There is no communication possible between you and the Asher, but you often experience the fact that you have one, just the same. You experience this as an impress of energy, or shall I say a *guardian angel* for spiritual safety. If I were to point out the presence of your Asher by using an example of stepping back on the curb when a car is about to hit you, you are most likely to ask me where the Asher was when you didn't step back on the curb and the car did hit you. The answer to such questions is that the Universal Law of non-interference is operative everywhere and all the time. In your knowledge gathering experience, you have the right (and responsibility) to exercise your free will. You will learn to pay attention to this impress of energy either on the curb or on the ground in the middle of the street. The Asher surrounds you as an energy vortex but such protection does not preclude your learning opportunities, so this arrangement is necessary. The Asher is not a member of your *Band of Associates*. Your personal Asher is not known to your band, nor does your band know the Asher since the lines of administration are different. Your Asher does whatever can be done on the astral level to fight your so-called battles there. So now, let's get into some specifics about the technicians that do comprise your *Band of Associates*.

2. Your *Band of Associates*

Each *Band* is made up of specialists and is predicated upon your basic need. This depends upon knowledge and degree of awareness. Before we go any further, I need to mention that when you pass over, your band is no longer under assignment to you. There is the Chief that is responsible for the operation of the group. Most of the time, communication to you is from the group Chief that takes information from all the other specialized technicians in your *Band*. The information is then distilled into some kind of form and given to you at the level and in the way you can accept it. That might mean a phone call at exactly the right time or an insight regarding something you needed to know and just couldn't figure out.

The Chief is the spiritual technician and acts as the Gatekeeper to call upon one of the other technicians needed to get the information out and through to you. It must be an impress of energy in such a way that you can accept at the time. When you make contact, it is most likely the Chief you are aware of and experience through your intuitive development.

Another volunteer, the Karmic Technician, oversees the Law of Cause and Effect in the outworkings of your spiritual growth and Universal awareness. A Creative Technician is consulted about how you are going to manifest your creativity, and a Timing Technician is consulted about the timing of events needed for you to accomplish what you need to do in order to learn, grow, and develop. In other words, what you intended to do once you incarnated.

The Chief, as Gatekeeper, the Karmic Technician, The Creative Technician, and the Timing Technician are the basic qualified volunteers that comprise your *Band of Associates*.

Levels in the Hierarchy

The level that exists above your *Band of Associates* is a Teacher Group. There are about six to eight teachers in every teacher grouping. These are highly trained technicians in energy performance, karmic outline, and karmic needs. They are directly connected to the band, not directly to each of us as individuals. However, individual problems can be passed directly to the teachers through the band and answers are forthcoming. The impress from the Teacher Group is one of awareness of Universal Law and application to oneself.

The level that exists above the Teacher Group is the Reincarnation Board made up of teacher-guides as technicians and reviewers. You go before the Reincarnation Board technicians to ask permission to reincarnate. It is here that your blueprint is drawn up and presented to you for your approval. Your genetic needs and your astral release timing are assessed here in miniscule detail.

Reincarnation Board Considerations

The balance of our planet is made up with one-half of the individuals incarnated on earth setting in a background life (an equation to be solved in the next lifetime) and one-half of the individuals on the earth who are aware of their background lives and have incarnated with the answer to their learning equation. Just as you can't write the equation at the same time you are solving it, so it is with a background life and the subsequent solution life. Consider that when you are setting in a background life, you are given a script with only your lines on it, knowing nothing else throughout that lifetime. However, when you incarnate into your learning lesson life (as a result of that background lifetime), you are given the whole script to use with all the parts you are designed to play.

For some time now, the Far East and the Middle East have been on background lives, while the western part of the globe has been living out solution lives. Look and see what occurs when we go over and try to help these people from our standpoint of solutions. It doesn't work out well at all because they are in the process of setting in the equation to be solved during their next lifetime. They don't want our solutions. This is a very simplified explanation of the essence of a much more detailed situation.

Types of Incarnations

The following are some examples of the types of incarnations considered by the Reincarnation Board:

1. Learner. The majority of people are in this state. There is a background life that sets in an 'equation' followed by the solution life that offers the opportunities to solve the 'equation'. The ideal situation is a 1:1 ratio, with one background life followed by one solution life.
2. Student-Contributor. This deals with the individual's own life learning experience, and then in later years they make definite contributions. As they become efficient learners, they offer contributions as an example of learning.
3. Contributor. From their earliest days, the individual makes a major contribution. This could be a deformed body in order to aid society in learning, but it can be in any number of ways.
4. Stacking Lives. These are lives where individuals become distracted and pre-occupied with circumstances that have nothing to do with their reason for incarnating, so they keep coming back to solve the same 'equation' over and over again.
5. First timers. These individuals are making a major adjustment in a physical body in order to learn proficiency with body requirements. They must learn to understand the five physical senses throughout their nervous systems. All first-timers are inclined to try to pull away from their physical bodies and start living in their heads. Ninety-eight percent of them come in as female, but both male and female are in a non-competitive position. They are all very intelligent with obvious creative talent, although not necessarily artistic talent.

6. Root racers. A root racer was assigned to the planet when the planet had consciousness assigned to it, and they will be here when the planet finishes with its assignment. They go to other galaxies and come back and forth to earth. They reflect the general state of the planet physically and mentally and are rather ponderous in reflecting mass consciousness with simple, mundane, and materialistic interests. They may be very creative, but they are basically not spiritually oriented.

The Council Level

The level that exists above the Reincarnation Board is the Council. There is no chance of individuals dealing directly with the Council. The members of the Council advance from the Reincarnation Board and have, among their responsibilities, the responsibility for etheric roadways and other celestial activities. Simply put, these technicians have the intelligence to make sure galaxies do not bump into one another. All members of the Council passed certain requirements from the Teacher Group to the Council level with a high state of awareness. The Council Chiefs have enormous capacities. Jesus was a former Council Chief. When a member of the Council incarnates, personal experiences are laid out heavily in the early part of life for that person. In order not to ignore the karma of human form, the Council member gets deeply involved in the assigned work area.

The Master Level

The level that exists directly above the Council is made up of three Masters. Once at the Master level, an individual does not reincarnate. All three were former Council Chiefs, and they were elected by the Council. Each of them is responsible for one-third of the world's operation and they work through the Council.

The Avatar Grouping

The level that exists above the three Masters is the Avatar Grouping elected from the three Master's level. Just as there is an Avatar Grouping for Planet Earth, there is an Avatar Grouping for every planet and an Avatar Grouping for every galaxy. There is also an Avatar Grouping in charge of all the Avatar Groups in the galaxy. The Avatar is the closest to our God concept. The frequency rate is so high that the degree of light is overwhelming. The circuitry from the Avatar level to us directly could not be sustained by us. There is a limit to the frequency you can generate from earth's frequency to the Avatar level. For that reason, there is no direct contact. However, we are all tied together in this whole complex system that is constructed for each of our benefits. Awareness increases step-by-step as you work on yourself, until you habitually feel the unity. That is <u>the</u> sense of unity.

You garner benefits from whatever you face in your life in terms of growth. There are very definite things to be aware of on the non-physical level, just as there are on the physical level. Be aware that consciousness permeates all levels that we can find, which includes the negative, opposing forces to the positive. Individual consciousness that is primarily ruled by the ego is not for human good and is devilish. Selfish interest is the indicator. Attitudes (pro and con) and decisions determine the difference between negative and positive. The negativity shares side-by-side with the positive. Neither will be left unattended.

All things work in harmonious balance in the Universal Plan, and each of us is a determining factor on how the Universe goes. There are two colors in the Universe in equal amounts. They are black and white. This is something to look at in terms of consciousness operating in an intelligent manner in a particular form. So, what do we have here? Person A and Person B. Person A chooses to love you and is kind, understanding, and patient. Person B chooses to kill you with words and deeds for their own self aggrandizement. Both are based on Universal Law. In order to grow, the determination is ours.

Yes, you are assigned a positive *Band of Associates*, but you cannot ignore the positive and negative elements. The negative is out after its own personal agenda and joins together in lower levels. Remember, nothing changes in consciousness when you make the transition and die. The Universe is infinitely perfect, and Universal Intelligence does operate. It does have Its form.

The Avatar Concept

The problem with the Avatar concept is that it is just simply not understood. Therefore, it is never looked upon in its proper aspect. People either go to one extreme or the other. Yes, this is God incarnate or not, but it is what is meant by the relationship between man and God. What I want to do is to bring this down and expose both ideas to you to the point where maybe you can make up your own mind.

Mythology

There is a great deal to consider when you consider the whole Avatar structure and the Avatar philosophy. In the

Hindu philosophy, it simply means a God coming into an incarnation. This Avatar idea is something that has gone on for a long, long time. The ancient Greeks and the ancient Romans had a very involved structure in mythology regarding the Avatar theory. For ages it was believed that the only way man came into being was through the incarnation of God. God looked favorably (or unfavorably) upon mortals and, in many situations, a female was chosen to be the wife of one of the gods. In ancient times, the mystical rituals were set up around the whole structure of fertility.

The concept was that humans were so far below the level of God that man had to work out some kind of arrangement to incur the favor of the Avatar, the favor of God. The basis of religion in early times was that nothing was more important than fertility. Fertility included having many children, but it did not just mean populating the earth with them. The concept was that the fertility of the land would die off and there would be famine, floods, and pestilence unless man could bring the Avatar down in some shape or form.

The whole basis of current day religion is based on the idea of God being an Avatar incarnated in some basic form. No matter what religion or philosophy we go to, we find this message. The American Indians, for example, had a God of air and a God of fire, a Spirit of the seas and a Spirit of the mountains. This concept was in those things man found tangible, practical, and material from the Avatar as God.

What we need to understand from the very onset is that without this concept there is no basis for Christianity, Hinduism, Buddhism, mysticism, or what have you. All of these are based on the concept of some infusion with God to man, some infusion from an Avatar at the physical level. You can go as far back as very ancient oriental philosophies and find very definite aspects to indicate that man cannot get along by himself. The concept is that man needs this idea of a God incarnate to fulfill the plan that man is not capable of handling himself.

Some current religions and philosophies have taken this avatar idea and badly misused it. For example, there is the concept that God walked the earth; the Avatar comes down and is completely incarnate. According to some philosophies, one of you may be an Avatar. The man Jesus, Buddha, Mohammed, and a few others would all certainly be considered Avatars as gods incarnate. This can be right or wrong depending on how you look at it.

I would have you consider that the only place you have the idea of God as a human being is in mythology. We have no Avatars on this plane. In fact, you are not going to find an Avatar on any plane. The terminology is meant to be a sense of action, not a person. If you ever intend to do any reading along these lines, it is important to understand a very important point. Avatar is not a person. Avatar is a sense of action. It is the *essence* of some form of God incarnating, but not a form of **a** God incarnating in the form of man.

The Divinity of Man

In this concept, we have to discuss the idea of the divinity of man and that relationship to this particular planet. We read in *The Bible*: *Then God said, Let us make man in our image and in our likeness.** Those of you who have taken my Genesis class will find this familiar. Nevertheless, we have to go over it again because it is an integral part of the Avatar concept.

---

*Genesis 2: verse 26

The situation here is the fact that God (capital 'G') never did make man. Man is the outpouring of Original Consciousness, an original idea, and this original idea never had a beginning because there is only infinitude in the Universe. God did not start. Therefore, He can never end. It is like standing in front of a mirror with a mirror behind you. You look at your reflection and you keep seeing a row of reflections that keep going on and on. You can't find a beginning. There is just a row of reflections coming and going. This constant reflection of action is somewhat the relation of God to the Universe. It is impossible for you (or for anyone) to trace any of this back to origin. There is no origin to the Universe because there is no origin to infinity.

Nothing can be a <u>direct</u> cause of anything that is infinite. It has to be a part of something. If there ever was a beginning in a Universe this size (which there wasn't but if you think of a beginning), there was one initial implosion-explosion idea, and there you were. Do you see how inconceivable that is? Your mind cannot quite grasp how anything cannot have a beginning, so this continues to be an immensely confusing thing. Nevertheless, confusing or not (in this particular regard) nothing had a start. Under the idea of a complete actuality, nothing had a start.

Man's relationship to God is not God <u>and</u> man because the unity is the unity of consciousness. God exists. You exist as consciousness. It is as simple as that, and you can't go any further. What we see as you is an action of consciousness. My body is not a cause. It is an effect of a cause. You sit there as an effect of a cause. You can give yourself a name that you like, and you can build up a whole activity of experiences. In an ego sense you can say, "This is me. This is something that I did." These are nothing more than effects of Original Cause and Original Cause continuing as a unity of consciousness.

The interesting thing about Original Cause is that It creates. It has to create. That is all It does, and this is all that you ever do when you are living. You just constantly create, and it doesn't make any difference how mundane that may be. You might create a dinner, a dress, a painting, or you might create a business deal. It really doesn't make much difference. Creation, or creativity, is the basic action of consciousness of this Original Cause. When consciousness works in its basic form, it will constantly create. It cannot stop. That would be like saying, "Here, we can make God stop. We can make time or movement in the Universe stand still." Absolutely nothing in the Universe stands still. The molecules in your body and in the air are in constant motion. Because consciousness is in constant motion, it constantly creates. If we leave something tangible alone long enough, it will create itself into dust, won't it? Sure it will. It will begin to rot out. Your body does the same thing. Everything around you is in this constant motion.

Getting back to this idea of a God-man relationship. There was not this idea of God and then the idea where God says, "I am going to make man." *The Bible* isn't even written this way. I have already mentioned *The Bible* passage: "*Let **us** make man in **our** image and in **our** likeness.* Here is where the Avatar theory comes in. Avatar should be synonymous to mean god with a little 'g'. What is the difference between a big 'G' God and a little 'g' god? There is not any difference, except the idea of a big 'G' God (Jehovah or other names to other people) is the Original Cause behind the Universe. If we can put this into terms our minds can understand, there is one big God creating the Universe, and those things He creates continue to co-create with Him.

This is where the idea of co-creation comes in with one big God and continually little gods. Jesus said the same thing, did he not? Maybe he said it a lot simpler than I am giving it to you, but he said something like, "*Ye are gods and ye know it not.*" This has been a teaching throughout all time. Why don't you know it? You don't know it because you don't understand that in the original creative force, that which creates is constantly going on as a Creative Force. This constant Creative Force that goes on is the Avatar Force - little gods constantly creating.

This simply means that *every* planet in the Universe has assigned to it an *individual* of responsibility, a consciousness of responsibility. We have a concept in our way of living which leads us to believe that the Universe is full of holes. We say that we have life on earth but not on the moon, sun, Mars, or Jupiter, and not in other solar systems. Yet, aren't we finding out every day that this limited concept is more and more wrong? Holding to this type of concept, we are getting further and further away from the truth.

Spiritual Mathematics

We have a Universe filled with constant life activity. If you observe a galaxy, or some of these quasi-stellar galaxies, we constantly find that they are formed by pieces being thrown off by existing stellar bodies. Now, whenever a piece of anything is thrown off in the Universe, something is immediately assigned to it. This gets us into an involvement that I call 'spiritual mathematics'. Nothing is thrown off by accident because nothing in the Universe runs by accident. Everything is set up according to a divine Plan. Everything is set up according to divine Law. What we can see are such things as the law of electricity, the law of gravity, and the law of mathematics. Our whole world runs on the basis of laws regarding certain things we know and certain things that follow under certain conditions.

The Universe runs the same way. It is not an accident that we have a planet and then, all of a sudden, we have spinning off from this planet another stellar body. That is by design. When this happens, a consciousness of responsibility is immediately assigned to that stellar body. The spinning off of one little body from this mother planet is nothing more than a continuation of a creative idea. It may take a few billion years for it to happen, or it may take a few eternities as we know it, but it does happen in its own proper time. If it were left alone, what we would have is a Universe with all these parts floating around with absolutely no system to them, and this does not happen. As you know, consciousness permeates *everything* in the Universe. Therefore, it permeates little parts of planetary matter as much as it permeates the air around us. The permeation of this energy is what we call consciousness. Consciousness has a responsibility, and that responsibility immediately comes under the responsibility of what we call little 'g' gods, the Avatar responsibility.

This is the Avatar concept now going to work. Every planet that is formed has assigned to it an Avatar. Now, do we correctly say *an* avatar? No, it has got to be plural. The only thing in the Universe that can create singularly is God, Original Cause. That means the Original Cause, capital 'G' God, is all that creates as a singular entity. Everything else creates by plurality and unity. You and I do not create as individuals. You see, I don't create this presentation. It is created in concert with others. Actually, you participate in it and help create it. When you create in your garden, do you create that garden singularly? Of course not. The seed grower has some affect, and Nature has Her hand in it. It isn't your garden. You didn't *create* that garden. When you bake a loaf of bread, did you create that loaf of bread? Of course, you didn't. You had co-creators. The person who grew the wheat and the person who milled the wheat for you and turned it into flour, the truck drivers who brought the flour to the store, and the grocery who sold the flour to you all co-created with you.

The Unity of Creation

You are part of a group unity of creation. This is important to remember. Nothing in the Universe is created on a singular basis except original First Cause, where God, the intelligent First Cause Mind, is involved. Everything else is done by concert and unity. This is why we don't assign **an** avatar to a planet. We must assign a plurality, avatars, a group of creators. Why a group? Because one of the things behind Original First Cause in this idea of creativity is infinite creativity. In order to cover everything in the Universe in an unlimited way, God has got to be an unlimited God. We cannot just have one color or one paintbrush. We cannot have just one color of ocean, or just one piece of ocean, or just one piece of land. Everything must be done in such great multiplicity in order to maintain infinitude in the Universe. That infinitude must be maintained, otherwise we don't have a Universe. If there was any way to break the infinitude of the Universe, we would call it quits. If we destroyed any part of Its infinitude, the Universe would immediately be destroyed, and we wouldn't last one second beyond that.

Any part of creation cannot create something of multiplicity unless you create it with multiplicity. When we design a new planet or start anything in the Universe (and right now we are talking about planets – primarily earth) it must be done as a group unity with avatar(s) in order to contribute the necessary ingredients for that particular planet. Is earth not a planet of multiplicity? What are the three multiple factors on this planet? Those of you who have heard me for so long ought to have this down pat – spirit, mind, and body. Earth is a planet of trilogy. This is a three-unit planet in that particular regard.

Wherever we go on the planet, the three things that exist are spirit, mind, and body. No <u>one</u> person can create spirit, mind, and body. Only God, Original Cause, can do that but, right now, we are not talking about Original Cause. We are talking about the responsibility and the co-creative effort that took place when this planet started its formation. Just as one woman cannot bake a loaf of bread, it takes a unity of ingredients to bake a loaf of bread. You may be the one to stir it up and slip it into the oven, but you are part of a team.

Assigned to earth is this grouping in order to give to the earth the necessary factors of its multiplicity. The avatar factors of the multiplicity on earth are the essence of spirit, mind, and body. In other words, what we needed was an avatar grouping wise enough, capable enough, and creative enough to fulfill all the possible aspects of spirit, mind, and body for this particular planet. These things have got to be infused in the planet to begin with. We are not a product in the way we would like to think of ourselves as a product of God directly. We are a product of the planet on which we live. The perfection that we talk about is part of the unity of the globe as well as part of the unity of the individual.

This may be a shock to some of you, but nonetheless, understanding this helps you bring it into reality more than not. When the planet is forming, it has to have certain basic characteristics that it will carry with it as long as it stays in existence. When you are baking a loaf of bread, does it not have the basic characteristics that you add to it? Of course, it does. Some of you would add just a little more salt, and some of you may want to make rye bread. You would use rye flour, or some of you would use white or whole-wheat flour. Some of you might sprinkle sesame seeds on top. These are all loaves of bread, are they not?

Each has definite ingredients and definite characteristics that give your little touch to the loaf of bread. No matter what you do, you do the same thing. If you made five dresses, you wouldn't stitch all five exactly the same. A man goes out into his workshop and turns pieces of cabinetry. They never turn out exactly the same, even when he turns them out with machinery. Everything is just a little bit different in characteristics. The things you create have some basic characteristics from you.

On a planet, it is much more important than that. In the beginning of a planet, the avatars must infuse the planet with their basic characteristics. It is not a question of how many avatars form the earth. I can tell you right now that we had to have at least three. You can look at you and you can look at me. We can see there are spirit, mind, and body so, there are three basic characteristics contained on this planet. We had to have at least three avatars in connection with the planet: one an expert in spirit, one an expert in what we call mind, and one in the physical essences or what we call body. This was necessary in order for each one of them to give their basic characteristics to the formation of the planet. This is exactly what is done.

This is not a question of God creating man. It is a question, going back again to the first chapter of Genesis in *The Bible*, of *Let **us** make man, in **our** likeness and in **our** image*. What is the image and likeness of the avatars? Spirit, mind, and body. Each one of these avatars probably had to incorporate a number of aspects under each idea in order to make sure that everyone of us would remain individual. In other words, no direct repetition. No two are exactly the same. None of you have the same fingerprints. In all of the people who have ever lived, there has never been duplicate fingerprints or duplicate anything in either spirit mind or body. Each one of you has a different spiritual and karmic background, each one of you has different creative mind capabilities, and each one of you is different physically. There is not a duplicate anywhere in this world, and <u>there never has been.</u>

Consequently, the most wonderful part of this is that the creative avatar grouping that is responsible for this planet (and infused the planet with their basic characteristics) was such to make sure that infinitude remains. In other words, it, in itself, was an infinite grouping. As I have said, we had to have at least three avatars. Undoubtedly, there were more than three. There could have been seven or eight, or even more, but the point is they had to be present in order to bring these characteristics into the basic elements of the earth. From these characteristics you have come, and from these characteristics you shall return because you have inherited the characteristics of the planet.

When you are dead, you do not have a physical body, but you do have a body that you can portray. If you are really good at it, you can portray it in enough solidarity to make it known. If you don't think you can, you will soon learn in one of your incarnations or one of your departures here that it can be done. The point is, as long as you are connected to this planet, you don't lose the basic characteristics of the avatars that set it up. The theory being that as long as the avatar grouping infused the planet with their basic characteristics, all who inhabit it will inhabit those characteristics that remain. Obviously, they had to be good guys and not bad guys because all the characteristics had to be positive not negative. Therefore, whatever you have done in the way of negativity is nothing more than a build-up of the erroneous idea of these basic characteristics or a misuse of them.

Let's go back to the loaf of bread. If you follow a recipe when you are baking a loaf of bread, and that recipe is like the spiritual law set up by the avatars, your loaf will come out satisfactory and edible, assuming everything is okay with your oven. If you don't follow the recipe (which you have a right to do), it may not be very good or come out at all. This is all that man has done. Instead of using the basic ingredients that belong to the earth, he has decided to take away or add other ingredients that have changed the loaf of the bread of life. He is not getting a good loaf. He is getting a bad loaf. It is as simple as this.

Additionally, this concept applied with avatar characteristics says basically that everything the avatars must give a planet in the way of characteristics is given. Consequently, the planet contains everything necessary for the maintenance of the individuals on that planet. The idea of us seeking outside conditions is the greatest step away from our well being in the world. All of our healing properties necessary to maintain the physical aspects are here. The fuel to run our automobiles is here. The fuel to run our rockets is here. What we need to build our houses is here. Everything we could possibly need to keep going and to bring forth the positive basic characteristics of the avatars that set up the planet is already here, and they are here in their natural state available to everyone to be discovered. We have discovered some of them and some we haven't.

Fuel is made from things in their natural state. Houses are made from things in their natural state. Every possible thing you could ever want is already here and is available to everyone. It has been infused into the planet as its basic characteristic. This is why the use of unnatural food that has lost its natural aspect is a reversal of the basic avatar characteristic of well being for the body. The basic elements have either been destroyed or reduced to a bare minimum. There is a big difference between taking a natural grain and eating it, and then taking one that has been processed and re-processed without the basic elements to maintain it at the level it should be.

With this avatar grouping, I want you to remember that the planet is infused with the characteristic personalities of the grouping, but not of <u>an</u> individual avatar. This is very, very important because each one of us has assumed a part of that personality. This is not a copy idea that we are becoming just like one. It is the idea that we are using part of that personality while we are here. You need to go back to the original concept that there is only one original creation, one original God Thinker. The rest of us are all the co-creative action of that one Original Thought. We are equal to the avatars and we take on their basic characteristics.

Let me liken this to a home condition with children. Each one of the children is an individual by themselves, but don't they take on family characteristics by being around the family unit? They pick up family habits and, most of all, the way the family talks. You can even hear similar inflections in their voices, but that does not change their individuality. Man does the same thing. What we are exhibiting on this planet are some basic characteristics of the avatars that set up and maintain the planet. As such, you are all gods. *Know ye not that ye are all gods?* You are all avatars, and you are all gods incarnated because what you have brought into this whole system is the fact that you are displaying these basic god-like avatar characteristics. You use and display the characteristics of the avatars that set up the planet and infused their characteristics into the planet.

Are you gods? Yes. Number one, you are gods in yourself from the basic First Cause. Number two, you are gods with the characteristics of these avatars, which include the planet's basic characteristics. The idea that mankind is god-incarnated as an avatar has a great deal of reason. It is not a fallacy, at all. It means you exist in a unity, a concert of consciousness that allows you to employ and garner the benefits of characteristics far beyond those which we seem to be able to utilize on this particular plane.

The unity is not something way out in the Universe. How could you, in a finite sense, ever get a proper feeling in relationship to a God that is infinite and way outside of you? I would say that even a God that *could* set something like that up would be a God with a very weird sense of humor. Why would a God of infinite wisdom place you here and at the same time say, "If you ever want to get back to Me, you have to go somewhere else? If you have to go somewhere else, why are you placed here to begin with? It couldn't be in order to extend your reach because you belong to the great infinite unity. Therefore, this isn't a question of extending your reach. Working outside of oneself is why people do not do well in just plain living.

In other words, those god-like characteristics that are available to you are all the basic characteristics that the avatars infused in the formation of this particular earth in spirit, mind, and body. All of these characteristics are poured forth into the planet and become the basic characteristics of the planet in the ground, under the waters, and in the natural things that are grown. These characteristics are also in the body of man. Since all of this is infused where you live and within you, where would you go to contact 'God'? You would go to the only place you have to go which is right where you are. The basic characteristics you are trying to capture and employ already exist right here like everything else does. You are trying to capture the basic avatar characteristics or, in another term, the god-like characteristics of the formation of this planet. Why seek it elsewhere? First of all, it exists inside of you. If you can't find it inside of you, find it in the things of the planet. It exists in the ground. It exists in the trees. It exists in the ocean.

I was recently meeting with some young people in a group of teenagers. We got to talking about the idea of the spirituality of water and how it holds vibration. We got to talking about how people like to go to the seashore for a vacation to re-seed their spiritual being. Some people like to be near the mountains and the trees. In every single case, all people are trying to do is to bring themselves in closer contact with the basic elementary spiritual characteristics already infused in the natural surroundings. In those places, people seem to vibrate and come into concert with some of their spiritual characteristics located in those particular places.

The Law of Action

When you seek 'God', you cannot go out into the Universe to look for Him. He is there, but that isn't going to do you any good in your growth. You have to go along with the basic law of action as it has been set up for this planet. Look for the characteristics that have been infused here. The idea of meditation is not to end up in some state of Nirvana or some state of great feeling and wonderment. Rather, it is to come into concert with those avatar characteristics that are built into you and this place we call earth. This is what we talk about when we talk about unity and harmony with people. We are brothers and sisters under the skin because we all share the characteristics infused in the planet. We are all unity because, in consciousness, we share the basic characteristics of the avatars that connect us in spirit, mind, and body.

In other presentations, you have heard me mention the term 'avatar' using it singular in which I have stated that for each planet there is an avatar. This is true, but it is also untrue in as much as every planet has more than one avatar. There is a grouping, but I sense that to go into this type of consideration every time avatar is mentioned is too difficult. If you will look at it as if an avatar Chief represents the group unity of avatars, avatar can be represented as one. It is as simple as that. To the earth there is an avatar. To the moon there is an avatar. To Mars there is an avatar. In each case, the avatar represents a grouping. Whatever that grouping may be, the group infuses that particular planet with whatever those characteristics are. Very solid bodies could be found on the moon, very definitely, but I don't know that we will discover them because of the way we are acting.

Seeking

I hope I have covered well enough that the search for your spirituality cannot be outside of you. It has to <u>first</u> be inside, inner as it were. The Greek philosophies that say, "Go within" have a lot of understanding if they really know what they are talking about. You are trying to uncover those basic avatar characteristics (God-like characteristics) of your own planet from within yourself. From there you can move outward from inside-out, if you so like. This is something you can always depend on.

We have a condition that we call avatar rays which are nothing more than levels of consciousness or levels of energy. When the avatars first established the planet, they established certain rays or levels of vibration that transmit to the planet their basic characteristics. The avatars connected to any one planet do not desert the planet and are there for as long as the planet is in existence. Their presence goes on for billions and billions of years. In fact, the extent of time a grouping of avatars is with a planet can stagger the imagination.

Finding

Here is what occurs. By vibration we have a planet that is infused with the basic characteristics of the avatar at the very beginning of its formation. If these vibratory forces were cut off, the planet would begin to operate much like a heating element or a light bulb. These energy characteristics would begin to form energy waves outside the planet that we find on our particular planet through our magnetic field, for one thing. Left alone, this would begin to diffuse the energy characteristics and over a long period of time the characteristics would weaken and become weaker and weaker. Finally, the characteristics would be gone from this planet. This cannot be allowed to happen. That would break up the whole system, the whole Law in the Universe.

What goes on is that the avatars are constantly replenishing these energy waves. This is the underlying idea of the Seven Rays, or The Light Rays that we find in many philosophies. We could go down the list a mile long of all the things these avatar energy waves have been called. It is nothing more than your avatar group operating, as they always must operate, from a given point constantly feeding these rays of characteristic energy into the planet to make sure the level of the planet does not fall below that which it should. If that should ever happen, life <u>as we know it</u> here in spirit, mind, and body could not be sustained.

Every time man goes off his rocker and starts a war and begins to kill himself off and sends hatred and fear and all these other negative things throughout consciousness, there is a necessity that becomes quite stringent. The rays coming out have to be stronger, and the energy coming out has to be stronger. These rays have to be strongly adjusted. This is the reason the avatars will send, as it were, messengers or assistants down to the planet. For instance, great people like

Jesus and great mystical teachers (and groups) will be sent to the planet in order to formulate inner groupings which allow for this transfer of energy throughout the planet.

When we have any one spot where there is a great deal of fear or a great deal of hatred, a block forms. Negativity never creates. It blocks, since negativity can't even create more negativity. Negativity can only maintain itself as negativity. In the same way, when a deep negative consciousness dies, it attracts all negative consciousness from the earth into a mass knot and forms a negative network – a block. These energy rays still come in but when they hit that block, man's negation is so strong that it blocks those energy waves that are positive and good. If the positive and good energy waves coming from the avatar level remained blocked, we would have a complete disruption on the planet. (You can read more in-depth details about this in *Life in the World Hereafter: The Journey Continues* by Gregge Tiffen.)

Messengers

To get over this disruption, messengers (such as mystical teachers and mystical groups) are sent that you probably never hear about. Networks are pre-set like electrical energy to offset points of negativity because every negative thought, feeling, and action blocks positive energy waves. There is a constant balancing battle going on that looks something like a see-saw action, and the avatars know this. What you find of spiritual characteristics on earth, you find in harmony to avatar groupings because the relationship to harmony is aligned with basic avatar characteristics. At that point, the frequencies are tuned in and *ye are as gods*.

Life is the result, an effect, of creative First Cause. In order to harmonize, we seek First Cause basic characteristics and avatar grouping characteristics. It is those positive acts of seeking that harmonize with avatar characteristics. Consciousness can stretch itself out infinitely. That is how it goes into another dimension strengthening itself with joy and lightness while expanding like bubbles from a child's blow wand. That is the energy that issues forth and creates. Recognizing this, you can begin a new spiritual path at any time.

Ponder that over a cup of tea.

Part II
Beyond Telepathy

> *The breath of life depends upon the harmony between the terminals of the mind and the proper area of the target.*
> *--GT*

People are afraid to let themselves go and use what they are. I don't necessarily mean acquiring anything beyond what they have, but just *using* what they already have in terms of mind power and the courage to get the methodologies that turn them into what they can be.

We all know the limitations we place on ourselves regarding our own mental prowess and wherewithal regarding our mental power. We honestly do know that we are infinitesimal compared to what we can be if we would just be what we are. In sharing this information about psychotelemetry, I am assuming you want it. I am going to give it to you exactly as it works, and whether you get any benefit from it or not is left up to your own application. Whether you use it or not is up to you. I admit it will take some extra effort on your part if you want it to work on a long term basis.

Telepathy

The first thing to understand is that we are not dealing with telepathy. Telepathy is a matter of one point influencing another point, or one point acting as a sending station to a receiving station (or vice-versa). In those situations, information is being transferred but not necessarily gathered. An example of telepathy would be my mind thoughts going to you as a receiving station for the sole purpose to influence you according to my thoughts. That may not necessarily be information gathering to you.

Telemetry

In the search to gather information, we are looking for a means of measurement without getting involved in all the surrounding obstacles or conditions. The space program coined the word 'telemetry' in terms of guidance systems. Using electronic methods, telemetry transmits and receives frequencies between two objects such as a satellite and a home station. It can determine certain values. This allows for the measurement of distance from an object and measures the angle between one point and another point. The conditions and methodology normally applied to 'telemetry' are going to be applied for our purposes here.

When talking about a telemetry station, the target and the station are set. They are both known points. The frequency can be determined by what the station and the target are trying to establish. The target area receives *some* information. That is not the purpose of psychotelemetry.

Before we go any further and as far as I am concerned, individuals do not have a mind. Mind is something that cannot be defined unless you want to consider it a function of the brain so then call it the brain. When I refer to mind (as it pertains to this discussion) I am asking you to consider mind as consciousness that is confined within an individual's physical vehicle.

Psychotelemetry

Psychotelemetry is the application of the basic premise of telemetry systems applied to an individual using consciousness or mind. Psychotelemetry works on the basis of an information gathering device. How can you use consciousness (or mind) to go where you want it to go? How can you acquire the information you want to acquire? How can you register that information so it becomes valuable and useful to you?

Comparisons

In psychotelemetry, one point is C (consciousness) and the target is often unknown and questionable. That is unlike the station and the target that is set in telemetry. All that is needed in telemetry is a set frequency to transmit and see what happens. However, the human being knows the mind but does not know the target and does not necessarily know the frequency rate. In most cases, the information seeker doesn't know what he or she is looking for. Sometimes they say something is wrong, but they don't know what it is that's wrong. *I have a problem, but I don't know how to solve it. Therefore, I don't know what target to go to.* That is a marked difference between the science of telemetry as it is used and psychotelemetry that can be considered a whole new field.

What we are up against at a point such as this is that in order for the mind to operate it cannot be at rest at any time. It cannot be a stationary point because it constantly needs to get information. The information it needs and gets is to let it know where it is. The telemetry station knows where it is, whereas the mind never knows where it is. It always needs reference points. In reality, we are looking at a mind that is seeking out targets in a number of directions. It knows not where, nor does it know what. Therefore, mind is more concerned with keeping on the move rather than being at any certain point. The mind itself is going out as a searching element. It is constantly floating. This is what gives us a whole new basis for psychotelemetry.

What is the function of the mind when it is involved in a searching effort to find out where it is and what it is? Some of the pitfalls in meditation, as it is practiced, are to still the mind and to put it at a point in which it rests immovable and hopefully immobile. If you can still the mind to such a point, it loses its contact. It knows not where it is. The mind has to have a target in order for it to identify itself and function, because it is an information gathering mechanism. Those targets have got to be there in order for the mind to move between one point A and target area point B. Somehow the mind has got to get over there.

Whereas a telemetry station is sending out a wave between two fixed points, a mind travels between its initial point to another point only to discover that where it is at one point is only another reference point to where it wants to go. Literally, what happens is that the mind moves from point to point and immediately upon arriving at one point realizes it must keep going. We find the mind must be on the move constantly, moving from point to target and to another point to target in order for it to gather information. The telemetric quality of the mind does not allow for it to become a stationary point. The only thing it realizes when it arrives at a target area is to realize that the distance between itself and wherever it wants to go is a point from where it finds itself and where it *needs* to be.

You can see it is important for you to understand that the mind must not be forced (or trained) to be still in order for you to be able to use the power of mind as a depository for wisdom and a means to gather information. The mind must not be allowed to become a fixed point, or we have a limited boxed-in mind inside an individual who represents himself as a mind who does not know who he is. You may know a person who has a very boxed-in attitude and is fixed in their opinions. These are people who do not know themselves and are not happy with themselves. Mainly at that point, they don't even care. They are not going anywhere. If they ever get to an original target area, there they stay. They never know anything beyond that point. You can find these people in every walk of life, from high professional jobs to government agencies. This may even be the guy down the street who is digging a ditch and whose mind is not gathering any more information. Considered in the same light, this is paralysis.

Basic Premise in Mysticism

A basic premise in mysticism is that knowledge is the only reason for life. The more you know, the more you know you need to know. Knowledge gathering is the sole purpose of psychotelemetry and the sole reason for consciousness operating as consciousness, or if you prefer 'mind', operating as mind on this particular earth plane. The whole purpose for life is to gather and register *usable* information and to be able to make something of it when and if you need it. There is nothing else to do here! That is it. I am not talking about the intellectual because that person is not necessarily gathering information at all. That person may just be taking in written words and stated facts that are gathered by other people who went out and got the information. None of that becomes a part of the intellectual's life. They don't know any more than when they started. The individual who gathers information to use in application becomes knowledgeable. The result is growth and development that is someday distilled into wisdom.

Parabolic

Unlike the radio set frequency in the telemetry station, mind operates as a moveable device. It is up to mind to go and get the information because it must, of its own nature, seek out information. It cannot wait for information to come to it. It is not really true that the Universe acts. The Universe reacts. Heaven reacts or God (if you prefer) reacts. We have to be the actors. It is a dastardly situation for you to say *In order for me to get where I am going, I am going to surrender to the Universe as all consciousness.* The Universe is not in an aggressive mode. It is always receptive energy. It is up to you to be moveable and to go out there and find what you want to find. You cannot wait and have information poured into you. You <u>must</u> go and get it. The Source is everything and anything. It can be a person you meet in a supermarket or a book that falls from the shelf and hits you on the head.

You cannot identify the Source, but you can identify a target, and the target can be anything you want to make it. For example, you see someone wearing a fascinating piece of clothing. You immediately ask, "Where did you get it and how much did it cost?" That is mind seeking out something it didn't know. On the way over to get the clothing, you run into someone you have not seen in five years who tells you something that changes your life for the next week. Everything leads to something else.

If there is anything to fear in life, it is physical, mental, spiritual stagnation as a lifestyle. The mind is parabolic like a radar screen. Part of a circle sends out signals from a frequency rate hoping to hit a target. As a result of the signals hitting a target, something is sent back that hits the parabola and registers. This is an ideal image of what the mind is. The mind is parabolic. It is non-selective. It does not know its target, it does not know where it is going, and it does not know the information it is getting back. As a result of reflection, more is received back than is usable. Target after target is sending back information so that all of a sudden the mind is inundated with reflected information. Since the mind didn't know what it intended to begin with, it received much more than it can use. All it knew was that it was searching.

The average individual is worn out and decides to shut down the mind. The mind turns off and does not send out any more signals because it is overwhelmed and doesn't know what to do with all it receives. The turn off isn't so much that the individual does not want to search, but that more is too much. However, there are methods to make what is received meaningful to you in order that you don't shut down. Otherwise, there is no more information and no more growth factors.

Techniques in Selection

Let's use the example of eighty dishes of food. It is all there to eat. The food you don't eat is garbage and is going to go to waste. The active mind in the parabolic sense is like trying to eat all those eighty dishes when it goes out there after all those targets. However, once it receives all 'eighty dishes' back it wants to throw up and rid itself even if it is good nutrition. Good nutrition, in this case, can even mean inspiration and good thoughts. The mind closes down and shrivels and so does the body. However, you cannot keep me from putting eighty dishes on the table. You can make a choice among those eighty dishes. How much do you want? Which ones do you need to ignore? The task of the mind is to know which targets it wants, what to get from the ones that seem to be worthwhile, and which ones to ignore. We have our work cut out for us.

How do we know what we need? How do I know what I am? It isn't that difficult unless we make a mountain out of a molehill and overstate situations. The Universe is a simple operation, and It only becomes complex when we refuse to accept its simplicity. Mind can know, and it does know. It knows how to select. In order for the mind to operate in a psychotelemetric way, it must first develop a technique of selection based on the mind's own requirements – nothing more and nothing less.

The mind has terminals just as the receiver terminals on computers that analyze based on data received. Computers can process an enormous amount of information at a very high speed just as the mind processes with its three terminals: the spiritual-mental, the mental-mental, and the physical-mental. Then there is one more terminal and that is the activator terminal. This is the methodology for the mind to get its information, and this is how it is going to be used.

Consider how much information hits the mind in any given day. How much of it is computed? How much is too much? The volume hitting these terminals is just clogging the circuitry preventing you from operating efficiently. You are prevented from functioning with the information that is vital and important to you. Therefore, you don't *do* anything. If you don't take it in and use it, there isn't any sense in taking information in at all. Traffic noise, billboards, radio, and television all beam more information at us than we possibly use. It turns out that the only thing we absorb is that which is the loudest, newest, or most emotionally charged and overwhelms the five physical senses. Otherwise, we tune out and shut off. We are in a constant battle by trying to stay alive as a mental individual who is capable of thinking, while our society is basically trying to keep us from thinking by overloading our circuits. This keeps us from identifying our target areas and computing the information that is important to us individually. That is dangerous and that is what is going on. Whatever causes us to shut down is our enemy.

Spiritual Terminal

The spiritual computer processes certain types of information. We have every right to live in the sense of letting consciousness operate. The first thing it processes is holistic information. This includes the total, infinite, and spiritual genetics of who and what you are. It is designed for such information, seeks it out, and stays away from specifics. It sees information in relation to all other points, all the way out to infinity. It is going outward and upward. The other thing the spiritual terminal processes is past, present, and future cycles, and it is the only part that can deal with cycles because real cycles are highly erratic. They do a lot of things that we do not expect.

The spiritual terminals deal with unlimited, infinity in a time frame capacity whereby no two cycles repeat themselves. It is only your spiritual terminal that can tell you where you are. Otherwise, how do you know you are where you are? You don't know. You have been told, but you must be somewhere so where are you? You have a time line that is not like anyone else's. You don't know what kind of time line I am on. You cannot even pick up that information about me. You can only pick that up for you as an individual. There are days that you should work and some days you should not work. The spiritual terminal is the only part of consciousness (what we have been calling 'mind') that can find and process that information.

The spiritual terminal can also process universal relationships. *Where am I in terms of the universal whole?* This is important because we must know where we are at all times in the sense of belonging to the Universe. This is not in relationship to society. We can drive each other crazy by constantly changing points. However, a person becomes a prisoner if we try to capture that person and make him or her be what we need them to be. That immediately cuts off their life and their animation of life.

Mental Terminal

The mental computer processes current life experiences recently acquired as knowledge and current obstacles. This is knowledge that has been added to you in this incarnation as well as applied knowledge. For example: 2 + 2. The mathematics you knew before you got here is instinctual mathematics. You knew relationship without defining it as such. Then you incarnate, and you must put 2 + 2 together. Whatever is required at that point is put into the mental terminal system. Current obstacles are processed also. What is preventing you from going, being, doing where you want to go? The only obstacle is something that has developed in the last twenty-four hours, because there is no such thing as an old obstacle. You regenerate and give birth to old obstacles, but they do not exist beyond twenty-four hours. The rule of thumb is that if you cannot solve a problem in three minutes, you are to put it aside and stop thinking about it. It cannot be solved within that time frame. It will be solved at another time. Leave it alone if it cannot be solved immediately. Let it go.

Physical Terminal

The physical computer processes distance, size, and the existence of the target. It also processes information that concerns the stress of the body and the health of the body.

Am I alive or am I dead? It does this from the cells of your body. It is stamina that indicates if you are up to hitting the target and staying with it or not. Do you really want the information? Do you have the courage to hit the mark? It is longevity that indicates if you are going to last long enough to make the target a bit of usable information. This is minute-by-minute, hourly, and daily longevity. *I'll never get through all of this today* indicates stamina is going to end at zero before the job is finished. This happens when you don't want to do something.

The Activator Terminal

The activator terminal only works when the other three terminals match. Unrelated information cannot be processed because you cannot transmit three different frequencies. In other words, the activator terminal doesn't work when we try to process dissimilar information. The activator terminal registers similar experiences and stores that information. If it doesn't activate, we don't have the experience. If we don't have the experience, we don't store any knowledge. If we don't store any knowledge, we haven't learned anything. An experience does not necessarily have to be a physical happening. It is any knowledge that has been fed through the spiritual, mental, and physical terminals that activate the activator circuitry. Now it becomes a reality.

Without the knowledge, you are not having an experience. What goes wrong in life is you just go along bouncing from signal to signal. That can drive you crazy. You are not having an experience. You are having an upset and you cannot think. None of that gives you an experience. The psychotelemetric system works when you begin to gather, register and process information. *I want to know what information lies there that I need so that I can function and make an experience that adds to my knowledge.* You cut yourself off if you don't first have the experience of registering and processing the knowledge and then act based on that knowledge.

The point is that these computer terminals cannot process any information other than what they are designed to process. The spiritual cannot do the job of the mental terminal because we don't know how to separate the volume of information in a way that allows us to process it. We must know what each of these terminals process, and we must make sure that we process in that category or else we cannot have an experience. It is true that what someone tells you may trigger your curiosity to go out and have an experience.

Targets

Now we are going to turn to the quality of the target. Go back to simplicity. We are complex machines based on the most simple of terms. You cannot seek out target knowledge as a whole. You must seek it out in elements and process it in elements. What goes wrong is that we try to chase after knowledge and embrace it as if we are trying to consume a whole cake by assuming we can take one big bite and somewhere along the line that one big bite will digest the whole and work out well. No, it will not. In the same way, a problem must be broken down and dealt with in elements that work between your computer terminals and the target area. There isn't any other successful way of doing it. The more you try to deal with a problem, in totality, the more confusing it becomes. However, when you exercise some discipline and grit you are able and break it down into elements that you can seem to handle.

What we are dealing with in psychotelemetry is the ability

to deal with anything in terms of information gathering by learning how to do this as if it were second skin. We do this by getting the mind (consciousness) to function slowly in this area and then almost automatically. That way we can seek any target and immediately have the knowledge we want for the intended experience. Anything less than that has us bouncing around trying to find our way out of the forest.

Using psychotelemetry depends upon the harmony between the terminals of the mind and the proper target area. Therefore, we need to consider the target as a single mass made up of atoms and what the direct relationship of that is to the proton, neutron and electron of the atom within the spiritual, mental, and physical terminals.

The Atom

The atom is made up of three parts. There is the neutron, the proton, and electron. The proton is the positive charge of the atom. The neutron is the neutral part without any charge. The electron is the free agent spinning around the center mass. It is the electron, as the free spinning agent around the mass, that is the target area for the spiritual terminal. The proton, as the positive charge of the atom, is the target area for the mental terminal, and the neutron, as the neutral part of the atom, is the target area for the physical terminal.

In order for you to receive information from the target area, your spiritual, mental, and physical terminals must seek out and only receive the proton, neutron, or electron information from the target. The target has the two center areas of the proton and neutron, and it has the free agent spinning around it – the electron. The way you are built in consciousness is for the mental terminal to receive only proton (positive charged) information. The physical terminal receives only neutron (neutral) information. The spiritual terminal (the free agent spinning around the center mass) receives only electron information. In other words, you cannot match the spiritual terminal to the neutron of the target. You cannot match the physical terminal to the proton of the target. This is why the picture of the atom is an ideal visual to keep in mind.

Gathering Information

In order to gather information, you must hit the target with the appropriate part of the atomic structure. Information then flows so fast that you wouldn't believe it! That is what we call an experience. For the first time in your life, information really came in and it is a feeling that cannot be duplicated by any other method.

When the spiritual terminal hits the target area it receives information contained in the electron level on the outer spinning level. It wants the holistic pattern of the target. It wants the karma (the cause and effect) of the target. It wants the genetics of the target, and it wants the cyclic time of the target. The spiritual terminal seeks out only the target's universal relationship from the electron level.

Consider that all the targets are operating as a tri-level single mass. You don't ever want to try to force the three terminals in consciousness (the spiritual, mental, and physical) to gather information identically and simultaneously from the same level. If you focus all the terminals on just the proton of the target, nothing comes back to you. What you do is approach this sequentially and in order. Use the spiritual terminal to seek out what is spinning around the target. When you have the holistic pattern in relationship to the

Universe, you move to the center of the target and see what you get from the proton and mental area. The next step is to use the physical terminal by moving to the neutron of the target. In other words, if you are having a problem with a person, stop looking at the person as a person. Look at the person as an atomic mass. *I am going to turn each terminal on at each level to find out what is going on that I need to understand.* The person has no influence on you whatsoever as a person. Everything is reduced to its basic simple form. That is how you learn.

Consistent Resistance Factors

Here are some consistent obstacles for interference:

- The quality and condition of the consciousness (the mind station). If you are a negative person, in poor health, or wrapped up in tight frameworks, you are not qualified to go out and get the information. If that is the way you are going to be, then that is the way you are going to be. Otherwise, it is a matter of discipline.
- The confidence of the operator. We have been told for centuries that we are not qualified to get this information and that we need intermediaries. That is such a shame. There is something within us that knows we can do this and awakens the Sleeping Giant. You can do this, but you may not have the confidence to do it.
- The resistance of the human target. Human targets can produce a certain amount of resistance to any information gathering device. We can block one another off by never standing still because you can't hit a moving target. The more you are gathering information, the harder you are to hit. You are a

very poor target while others are trying to get you to stand still. As long as you keep growing, no one can really reach you. There is your answer. You are not a target for anyone.

Beyond Telepathy

We are not dealing with telepathy here, nor are we dealing with clairvoyance. In dealing with the basic rules of psychotelemetry, we don't want to know what something is, but we do want information from it. We approach the target as an atomic mass made up of the proton, neutron, and electron. Each one gives basic information that reduces everything to its basic simple form – the atom.

Part III
The Power of Observation

Words without deeds cannot affect the masses.
--GT

In an all intelligent Universe, a thinking Universe, there is a permeating and total Thought process occurring all of the time as basic raw energy. As one cell of the Universal body, each of us individualizes the Thought process and isolates a moment in infinity. The proof of that process is manifestation, which gives us two avenues: One is total omnipotence, and the second is the individualization (as part of total omnipotence) that we isolate and identify.

You and I are immersed in the Thought, and in order to pay attention, all we have to do is observe. This is not a head function. In an infinite thinking Universe, you do not concern yourself with the qualities of good or bad, right or wrong, negative or positive. You have no means by which to separate and evaluate these qualities because you cannot separate yourself from the sea of Thought. You and the Thought are the same thing. You can discover something no one else has discovered within Thought, but you cannot express it until you break away and become aware of what you see. Therefore, thinking is a two-fold element. One element is that you must not think. The other element is that you then think about what was there when you were not thinking in order to properly individualize thought.

Thought is energy and as an element of the Universe the energy is neutral. It must be observed as such. It is the observer's refusal to observe what he or she is observing that turns a thought negative. This is why the same thought can be negative to one person and positive to another. Fulfillment of the karmic process (i.e., the process of the cause and of that effect) can make the thought positive, even if it's painful.

To be an ideal thinker and garner the positive essence out of the Universal Thought process, you must extrapolate valuable meaning for yourself and then let the energy pass through you. This is essential albeit difficult to do. In order to be a selective receptor, you must determine what you do want and then let the rest of the energy flow by you.

Individualized Thought

Every thought has its polarity. Here is the process for evaluating a thought so that it may prove valuable and manifest on this planet:
1. Observe the thought.
2. Isolate it.
3. Capture it and keep all other thoughts out.
4. Enter into your thought process system, which is mental and physical.
5. Identify the thought through this process.
6. Manifest what you have identified.

The individualization process is one of expending energy in order to externalize (manifest) the thought but not to improve upon it. You cannot change thought or improve upon it because the purity is already there. Acceptance positions you to use the power. To be aware that the thought was always there and then to hold the thought in its natural purity in order to internalize and externalize it is a two-fold process.

There are few thinkers and a lot of talkers in our Western

society, which causes the non-thinker to become paralyzed. Ninety-eight percent of the people who are talking are not thinking, and two-percent of the people who are thinking are not talking. Without observers and listeners, we are destroying our society. We are becoming more communicative with volume but less understood. We are not capturing positive manifestation because volume is not intelligence. Volume simply increases the amount of noise added to the awareness process. This causes a spaghetti pattern. In this way, we lose ninety percent of the mental energy because it is wasted energy in an inefficient system. What is required is to emerge and be absorbed in the isolation of the Universally intelligent Thought.

Concentrated Energy

What I learned from my training in the Far East was to focus on a singular element and extrapolate energy from that element. It is quick once it is learned bit by bit, because total concentration does not take a long time. You get everything you need out of the element very quickly.

To even start the thought process, you need to become aware of what you think about most of the time. Every good thinker knows himself better than he knows anyone else. How do you turn a neutral thought into a positive or negative one? When you are aware, you are immersed in concentration and focused in thought. You must extrapolate (as if putting a frame around) the element that you want and those things that interest you.

The human mind is actually the thought process that permeates the physical unit from head to toe. It's not the brain, because every part of your body is a total thinking element, with the brain acting as merely a switching device through the nervous system into physical manifestation.

The Universal Flow

The Consciousness of the Universe and the consciousness of a person are inseparable. As I have already pointed out, your job is to individualize and isolate the element that you want through concentration. That unquestionably connects you to Universal flow because you are already plugged into an unlimited thought process. For example, something comes along, and you think you have reached a dead end. Mental fear has shut down your mind energy. Your fear is that the process has broken down, but the integrity of the system does not break down because consciousness is inseparable and unitized.

- The Universe is aware and Its parts do the thinking for It.
- The Universe is complete and knows Its polarities at all times.
- The Universe is aware and knows where It is and where It is going within any given point, but not as an ultimate destination.
- The Universe is impersonal, flexible, non-judgmental, and does not know Its polarities as good or bad. There are no loving or hateful thoughts. There *is* pure energy that is acceptable and just there.
- The Universe is subjective and objective. It is observable inside and outside of Itself. Therefore, you cannot run out of an answer or a thought. As individuals we immerse ourselves and let the thought process be what it is. It is by observation that the thought process shows itself.
- The Universe is analytical. It knows an infinite number of facets that are usable. For us to allow too

much volume equals a waste of time, which equals a waste of energy, which equals frustration.
- The Universe is Self-sufficient. We cannot improve on the Thought, but we can improve on externalizing what we have observed and identified.

Harmonious Interaction

The Universal Thought acts on information supplied to It by Its parts. Therefore, the individual is in control because the individual thought is fed to the Universe and informs the Universe of the individual thinking process. If we are constantly rehashing an old thinking process, we insure stagnation. The Universe cannot go into limbo because It is energy and movement. It must take action to sustain Itself. Remember: The Universe does not judge thought as good or bad. It will not alter any information we feed to It.

The Universe will protect Its own Law by realignment of Its parts. It cannot destroy Itself because that would be a violation of the Law. What happens is there might be a surge of energy to correct a deficiency in order to wipe out sick cells. Sick cells are the refusal to become aware of a new process, and this might mean that people or planets get wiped out. As individuals seek new elements of Thought and manifest these new elements, there is the universal harmony of harmonious interaction – the constant goal of Universal Thought form. You create by creating through a new thought process and breaking out of an old thought process. You do this by allowing yourself to move past thought barriers by looking for new elements.

When you have a bright idea, it registers in some part of your body because the magnetic structure of your skeletal system (every bone in your body) has a plus and minus polarity. You just brought in a vortex that will accept the character of a portion of the Thought that you magnetized. Your body was in accord with the Thought. Sometimes you might sense a portion of the Thought as a new thought and then lose it because your cells did not accept it. The thought bounces out from excitement, or the health of your body could not accept it, or there is fear that what you have identified as a thought will cause a change of some kind. That change will make you different from everyone else. Your cells may also reject a new thought if there is too much or too little to process.

Your body demands that the character of your thought goes to those cells where the thought was magnetically attracted in your body. This causes exhilaration. Then there is distribution, and your cells start the communication process. Your cells match their experience to the new discovery that is available in your experience. Your cells also determine which part of your body should take on responsibility for processing the new discovery. When that is done, the new information is correlated by your cells and fed directly into your nervous system. Your nervous system feeds to your brain, and your brain sends the information to the part of your body that is ready to receive the <u>new</u>. This is determined by the following:

1. The character of the new thought.
2. The part of your body that is responsible for manifesting the new thought.
3. The transmitting direction for the action such as your hands, voice, facial expression, or whatever part of your body received the thought.

Transmission

All your body cells went into the vortex to accept the new thought. When your body reached full awareness matched to the experience level, the thought was transmitted to your brain and the original vortex ceased to be. Your body is then in a receptive mode. Your brain transmits to the proper part of your body and that part of your body becomes responsible. It has to respond because it is in a receptive mode. To be able to act at that speed is the power of thought, and it is instantaneous. That is what causes you to speak, sing, dance, draw, write, or do whatever else might manifest.

At the point of manifestation, your will can prevent manifestation from occurring. The cells involved in the action contain historical information. And the reaction from that residual energy can shut down an action, even though the historical residual may be wrong because the brain cannot have input and output at the same time.

Changing Frequencies

This brings us to the point of being a co-creator. The process of self-containment is to allow the thought to happen and to be healthy enough to magnetize the Thought. For an individual to say, "This thought is mine" closes off co-creative energy. That is DANGER. An inventor knows when an invention is practical and leaves it alone. Know when the potential has manifested and been fulfilled. Know when to move on. In other words, your thought completes itself by going back into the Universe as part of the on-going Thought process.

New Aspects of Thought

People see a portion of the Thought brought into manifestation and that sends the portion of the Thought back to the Universe and moves the masses. The object of the thought process is to issue it forth and send it back into the Universe. Let it go. Get rid of it and go on. The change in you is a new aspect of Thought.

- You are a complete and powerful unit capable of walking into a sea of Thought.

- Take one drop and, through a series of activities, drop the Thought back into the sea by the doing, not by the thinking.

- Realize your basic power. Beware of lip service without understanding your power.

- Understand your part in infinity as your life, your continuity of thinking, and your actions. This is what it means to recognize your potential.

- To be a part of total potential, you must be willing to be responsible for the results. Make your move and see it through.

- Accept your responsibility, and do not wait when you need to act.

- Think and do. Turn what you have done over to the Universe. In so doing, you have to make adjustments in your life and correct your pathway. You are never the same again.

- Thinking creatively, people pour out energy without

ever stepping on other people's toes. They are always developing something new by adjusting and constantly making corrections.

When you know you cannot afford to be the same, you change. You become your own self-discoverer.

Part IV
The Ubiquitous Soul

> *You ride the winds of the Universe.*
> *--GT*

In contemporary metaphysics, there is an irritation that arises from the firm belief that what you are here on earth is not completely you. That belief indicates that there is an important part of you existing outside of you that has a definite effect on the operation of your activities. In this series, I hope to explode a few aspects of that belief.

First, we have the word 'soul' to consider. Your religious upbringing often determines the meaning of the 'soul' for you. Under certain orthodox philosophies, the idea of the soul is that pure divine part of you. It cannot to be touched in any way, shape, or form by any mundane living earth activity. It is considered to be that part of you that remains absolutely pure and absolutely spiritual in the Universe, and it goes on and on regardless of whether time goes on or not. The soul is considered to be that part of you that is a direct part of God and is life everlasting. You have heard it all.

Those humans who have the tendency to be quite negative feel that somehow it is a saving grace to have a soul identified as that one spot of purity they can fall back on. "Well, I have a soul, and my soul is untouched. I have a soul, and my soul can be saved regardless of all these terrible, negative, and sinful things that my mind and my body do. Still, my soul can be saved." You know what I mean. You have all come in contact with this in one form or another, in one religion or another, and in one philosophy or another. What an escape that is! It's as if the soul is that one bright little something which you are, but it doesn't seem to *do* anything. It doesn't seem to have any activity. It is just there. I don't like to think of you that way, and I don't think you like to think of yourself that way either.

Then we come up with the word 'spirit' that has caused an equal amount of confusion. As far as I am concerned, there is absolutely no difference between soul and spirit. Those who would argue differently would say that the soul is that divine spark that we have, but spirit is something that allows us to think. Most metaphysicians point out that this reference is to spirit when considering consciousness and divine Mind. Actually, we have a body that is the solid construction of the individual. Then, we have this thing we call 'spirit' or 'consciousness' that makes the body work. Within their theories is the belief that the soul has absolutely nothing to do with the mundane business of the body or the spirit of consciousness.

We have to be earnest about these things. First of all, when we talk about body, mind, and spirit where does soul fit in? It has to be the same thing as spirit. Mind is a very nebulous thing. Mind is not brain. Mind has to be the same thing as action. If mind is spirit, as many metaphysicians say, then you do not have a trilogy. Even a metaphysician cannot buy a philosophy without a trilogy.

The semantics date back even to the time before Moses. There are interchangeable terms for such words as love, god, spirit, Law, Lord God, angels, and even devil. All of these words meant the same thing depending upon how the writer wanted to use them, and nothing is going to change that. In modern times, we continue to have the same interchangeable terms with the words soul and spirit.

In a similar way, we can relate this to the way nuclear energy works. Scientists take plutonium and other necessary elements to make nuclear energy. We can say that the core of those elements is the soul. To illustrate this point, let's draw a circle and say the circle represents spirit. We can draw another circle within the first circle and say that represents the soul. If you really want to be honest about this, there is another element inside another element and inside yet another element, ad infinitum, until you finally realize you can never get down to one little neutron and proton of soul energy. This is also true on an individual basis where you cannot have just one little spot of identifiable soul energy.

Divine Action

What are people talking about when they are talking about soul and over-soul? The whole basis of the soul and over-soul discussion is based on the idea of control. To me, we need to be talking about *doing* something in a divine way. We need to be talking about action, so let's take a look at some of the important aspects of soul and over-soul.

Separation

First of all, mankind is trying to build a monument to stupidity and to their general ignorance by insisting that they remain separate. Everything that humans have ever done tends to breed division. They take a day and divide it into hours, and hours into minutes, and minutes into seconds. They take plots of land and the first thing they do is subdivide it. They build square houses because it is easy to divide squares into other squares. A person becomes obsessed with dividing himself and dividing everything around him. This need to separate also extends to the whole aspect of talking about God. Humans simply cannot take the aspect of God and leave it alone as a totality.

To say, "Within the totality of the Universe (or God, if you prefer) I exist, and I will leave it that way" indicates an understanding that at one point in time, there was just God. In Biblical terms, we recognize that point in time as the Garden of Eden. Then along comes the idea that there is God and there is man. Right away we have a separation, a division between God and man, instead of the original satisfaction with singularity and unity. At that point, man was no longer satisfied with the idea that man is part of the totality, which includes everything about himself and everything about the Universe around him. He had to take the position where he could put everything outside of himself and look at it. Why? The whys to these questions always come up with the same answer.

The answer is that man is so afraid of being responsible for his own mistakes that he realizes if he separates himself from something it gives him an out – at least he thinks it does. He can then always blame the thing that he says is not a part of him. Therefore, that which he has done is not his responsibility, but it is the result of this outside *thing*. This is the old business of the act of a cruel God who chastises and is a punishing God. That is man saying, "Look, I don't like the setup we have here. This whole idea in the unity that I am man and I am also God means if I do anything wrong, I won't have anyone to blame because I am all there is. Well, I can't live with that. I don't like that system, at all, because it doesn't give me a fall guy." He immediately puts God outside of himself and says, "Ah, now things are better. There is God and there is me. If things go wrong, I can blame it on God and not on me. Now, I am safe."

This is a very important point of awareness because it is this type of philosophy that has bred the concept of soul and over-soul (among other things). <u>I may as well tell you right up front that I don't believe a bit in a soul and over-soul.</u> That whole idea gives man an out and allows him to sit back and say, "I can get away with acting like this because there is something better outside of me." If there is one thing that causes the downfall of mankind in all forms (consciousness, mind, body, spirit, soul, or what have you), it is human's great desire to separate or to divide. Within the statement *United We Stand; Divided We Fall* is the whole key to spiritual awareness.

Individuality

Let's take the case of individuality. Somewhere down the line, we had a philosopher come along. Maybe he was wearing a fig leaf. He came up with the idea of man taken as a singular being who should exercise some individual action. In other words, he wasn't satisfied in saying, " In the Universe is a circle, and that entire circle is God." The philosopher didn't like that concept. Instead he said, " Oh, sure there is a God, but leave God in his heaven. I am an individual. I think, therefore, I am. Whatever else is outside of me, be it divine or be it human. The one thing I can always count on is that I am an individual."

It is this insistence on individuality that furthers the whole concept of separation. In separation, it isn't God in action. It is man in action. God helps every once in awhile, or man lets God help once in awhile. It is just such a philosophy that spawns the primary separation from the Source of all activity. Many of the philosophies and philosophers (I do not mean to infer all of them) embrace the idea of individuality and that man stands alone. As long as man thinks, he has the ability to stand alone barring any divine influence whatsoever. The soul and over-soul type supporters have taken the idea of individuality and turned it around. It is insidious the way this has built up.

Dependency

What seems to be a paradox, a reversal, is the concept of dependency along the lines of what I have already covered. The fact is that it was originally just God and man's being within God. However, man didn't like this idea either. In the same light, dependency grew. "If I can't live up to the rigors of life and am not willing to do anything, I can fall back on not doing anything, so God you do it. I am not worthy of anything." This is a bigger problem than you may think. We have people, more times than I care to think about, who get ahold of metaphysics and before you know it they have the idea that if you stand back and let God do everything, God *will do* everything. In theory that is an accurate concept, but in practice they truly don't know what they are talking about. What they are really doing is using the philosophy of dependency to uphold their own inaction. They don't *do* anything.

There was a report in London of a woman who was in all sorts of trouble, legal and otherwise. She turned to her minister for advice. He told her to just go home, don't do anything, read *The Bible*, and just stay out of the way. In other words, she was to *let go and let God*. She did this and in five days all of her affairs were straightened out to her satisfaction. This is true, but there is more to it.

The report does not tell you the state of this woman's consciousness during the time she was reading *The Bible*. It doesn't tell you a lot of things so people get ahold of this and say, "I don't have a job and things aren't going well. I have a wife and a youngster to raise, and I don't know what to do. I will just sit here and wait for God to do something." They put so much of their dependency on an outside influence that they, literally, become paralyzed and simply give up.

This is the kind of defeat that is within the realm of separation. It puts God within the circle and cuts Him in half saying, "Okay, here is one-half here (A) and another one-half there (B). B will not act until A does something, and A will not act until B does something. What happens? Nothing! This is what happens when man separates himself from God and waits for God to do something. Well, God under such conditions as an intelligent energy without emotions or feelings would wait for man to *do* something. Staying with this example, the minute man does something - anything! - God, Intelligent energy, gets to work because there is something to work on.

The dangerous philosophy of soul and over-soul says, "Here I am down here as soul and up there somewhere is over-soul. Therefore, if I don't know what to do I will sit and wait for over-soul above me (or wherever it happens to be) to do something." This dependency is based on the false idea that when you don't know what to do some wise over-soul, a God-like energy, will do something. At this point, what do we have? No energy flow! The idea of the soul and over-soul has a hold on so many people because it is presented in such a believable way. Nevertheless, when you realize what it is based upon, I deeply hope you will never again be enamored by such an idea.

Duality

Let's look at duality as another underlying factor of separation. However, I have already touched upon this subject somewhat. Man is designed as one, and the idea of one leaves man dependent upon himself. He is responsible to himself for both his so-called good and his so-called bad, but he doesn't admit this. He fights with every last ounce of his strength to eradicate his oneness. He brings in some kind of duality in order to separate and set himself apart, but he has no right to be separated. He belongs as one. For example, we know there is as much male energy within every female as there is female energy within every male.

I need to emphasize the problem with the illusion of duality that underwrites the soul and over-soul concept. Man is not satisfied to sit here and say, "Okay, here I am, and I have a soul. That soul is completely me." Instead, he insists on breaking it apart. Why does he insist on doing this? He does this because he will not face his own responsibility. The concept of soul and over-soul is a monument to ignorance and to the lack of courage.

Living a spiritual life is not always an easy proposition. It is very fulfilling and enjoyable but not necessarily easy. What humans are really faced with is an outrageous attitude. The minute you put the word 'and' between God 'and' me, <u>you</u> have caused the appearance of duality to take place. You eradicate the reality of the singular condition of unity. The minute you go back to the original beingness of man's oneness, the soul and over-soul concept is out the window. You can't have one and have two at the same time. One is one and that is all there is to it. Anytime you run into someone who says that they believe in the soul and over-soul, you can ask if they believe in the unity that God is in man and man is in God. They will say they do. How can they explain duality in soul and over-soul and still believe in unity? That is inconceivable. They are in opposition to one another.

Unity

Let's take a look at unity. I am endeavoring to explain the idea of unity in order to give you some grasp of unity in relationship to separation. How do you describe unity when you talk about God? As the metaphysical phrase goes, *God is a circle whose circumference is nowhere and whose center is everywhere.* There is no way of understanding this in the cold logic of mind.

The idea of unity is more of a *feeling* than it is an expression, or philosophy, or anything that can be put down in graphic form. Sooner or later in your pursuit, you eventually come to some basic idea that you live in this infinite Universe, and that life is an everlasting thing. Problems are nothing more than what helps you to produce your spiritual fiber. They are also everlasting. All sorts of things that you are faced with in your world today are everlasting. This is unity because everything is part of One. You don't exist. I don't exist. You sit there and say, "I am me. I can give you some substance of what I am." You absolutely cannot. All you can tell me is that you have recognition at this particular point in time of something sitting in a body that you are using. Period. You are used to its form, its weight, its feel, and its motion. This is all you can tell me about yourself, but you don't really exist. Universal Intelligence (God, if you like) exists. This is unity.

Man insists on the idea of separation. Generally speaking, he will not tolerate unity in his concept. Why? Because it means you are not rich or poor, you are not good looking and you are not ugly, you are not smart and you are not dumb. You are not liberal and you are not conservative, nor are you black, white, brown, or red. You, as the idea of man, are absolutely nothing. God is all things 'He' needs to be. This is so incomprehensible and such a threat to a person's ego, that those who advocate soul and over-soul are able to bring that philosophy into being. They say that the soul and over-soul are within the unity, but within the unity we separate ourselves. Take a good solid look at that concept with common sense. How can you separate something within the unity and still say you have unity? Unity is all-in-One. <u>Nothing</u> within unity can be separated.

There is a point in the Pacific Ocean off the coastline of Carmel, California, where the Japanese current and Alaskan current meet and join together in the ocean. Oceanography tells us that we have two currents coming together, but we can stand there and all we see is water. We can't tell one current from another by any change of color in the ocean. It is unity. Within the ocean, it is all water with many currents and many things going on. All of it belongs to the ocean. Within the Universe, there is God. That is unity. Within that unity you can say there is soul but the soul, in order to be the soul, *is* the soul. There is NO separation.

We cannot take one individual soul and separate it. That takes us back to the irreversible problem of separating something within the Universe. <u>That just cannot be done!</u> This whole idea is most likely difficult to wrestle with, so I suggest you write it down or highlight it and keep it around. It may take some careful deliberation on your part. Primarily, consider what you can do with unity. Absolutely NOTHING. This is the pure beauty behind the whole concept of God and the Universe. You cannot do a single thing to or with unity. One-is-one and there isn't anything you can do to it. You can't diminish it because it would then no longer be one. You can't add to it, or you no longer have one. When you have separation, you have two. What can you do to two? You can divide two, and you can subtract from it. You can do a lot of things to two.

I do not want to give you the impression that you don't have a soul or spirit. On the contrary, yes you do! However, what you <u>must understand</u> is the wide range of activity and capabilities of this soul of yours. Once you understand what the action of soul is, you can understand the *real* reason that soul and over-soul doesn't work and doesn't mean anything.

The Soul Memory Drum

Just as the soul within each of us is invisible, there is in each one of us what I like to call the soul memory drum. It is the most invisible thing you can possibly imagine. If we could draw it graphically, we would have a picture of highly active energy waves, much like electricity. These waves form certain patterns. Picture in your mind's eye something that looks like a flag. I like to use the image of a flag as a representation because there are many different colored threads that move in various ways. Within each one of you in this area of soul and spirit, you have this memory drum, which is not unlike a flag. It contains hundreds of trillions of billions (I don't know what the highest number could possibly be) of these energy waves all working into some kind of a pattern. If we must give it some identifiable shape, it is more oblong than it is square or rectangular. Don't worry about that for now.

This memory drum has two functions. One function of your memory drum is to record all your experience of the soul (or spirit) from the very time of inception. This is very important. When was the spirit born? Where was the beginning of the soul? <u>Here is the key</u>: Since you never had a beginning but, in fact, you began with God and God is immortal - God had no beginning and no end – there is immortality recorded within each one of you. It is the soul memory drum that records everything you ever have been, are, or will be. Therefore, this unity that we call 'God', this state of perfection, this immortality, this Alpha and Omega (no beginning and no end situation) exists within you. This is your major saving grace. You can't just sit back and say that things are pretty bad and that you doubt if you will ever reach perfection. It isn't a question of you reaching perfection. It is a question of recognizing what is already there.

Another function of the memory drum, and a very important one, is to leave a residue of energy of all these experiences wherever the soul has been. Look at it this way. Draw a long line as a representation of X number of years in length of time. Each indices mark along the line indicates an experience. Some marks indicate experiences in other galaxies or an experience in the discarnate state of being. Some marks indicate a female life and other marks indicate male lives incarnated upon the planet. Keep going as far and as long as you wish indicating different experiences along the line of infinity.

The energy of the soul imprints itself much like a copy machine upon the whole pattern in the Universe. The Universe is a tremendous, infinite, sensitive receptacle. Every time something happens with a soul, the soul does two things. First it records that incident into its own memory drum. Secondly, it flashes it like a picture would flash onto this tremendous screen within the whole Universe. What I am pointing out is that in the soul's travels, in the soul's experience, every place your soul has been, every place you have laid your foot (and wherever your soul has stopped along the way) you have left some residue of energy. This residual energy forms itself into another pattern and *always* exists. To give you some idea of the concept of the Universe: Every word you have ever spoken never dies. Every thought you have ever thought never dies. Wherever you have been, you have left an imprint, a soul imprint. Any time you ever start feeling lonely, think about that. Try placing the line back as far as your mind can possibly conceive and sense how many times, how many thoughts, how many actions, you have left behind.

These are the two functions of the soul. It serves as a memory drum for all the experiences of the soul, and it forms an energy soul imprint wherever it has gone. This is very, very important. As we go along, I will show you how this plays such a significant role. Meanwhile, remember that this affects every incarnation, every discarnate state, every planet, every galaxy, and every aspect of the Universe, no matter where you have been, who you have been, or whatever you have done. Consider in a more finite way that everyplace you have put your foot from the time you awakened this morning, and every place you have set your mind today has set your imprint. For this particular consideration only, your body is pretty immaterial. It is NOT immaterial as your vehicle for consciousness at this particular juncture, but we are setting it aside for this consideration <u>only.</u>

Without thinking about the people in your life for a moment, think of just yourself and this enormous infinite screen that is recording all of this. You, acting with this soul memory drum, are making a picture every place you go. How many did you make today? As you are thinking right now, you are making a set imprint. Now, multiply this by your incarnate and discarnate lives and extend those beyond your experiences on this planet into time immemorial. You have got muddy footprints *all over* this Universe.

Soul Mate Theory De-Bugged

I need to bring in this idea of the soul mate theory that simply states a man and a woman have a destiny together, and that they are divinely married in some heavenly way from the beginning of time because they are destined to be soul mates throughout all eternity. It is bondage to think of yourself tied and inseparable to some other soul. It is not freedom, and it doesn't hold water in any spiritual sense *at all*. According to the soul mate theory, it doesn't matter whether you are married to your soul-mate right now, or even if you have both incarnated at the same time. They say that along your line of experience and the other person's line of experience you are together. You may go through lives where you are not together. Then in other lives somewhere along the line of infinity you come back together again. The theory is that you come back together over and over again throughout eternity.

Unity <u>cannot</u> work under those terms. You are dividing yourself within unity and that <u>does</u> <u>not</u> work. A person may go to a 'psychic' and talk about a relationship problem. Most often, the 'psychic' says that is because they are soul mates working out some kind of karma. The whole theory being that they are inseparable. This is not true. What is true is that they have common goals. It's true that individuals have been brought together any number of times over and over again. One of the reasons they keep running into each other is that they have common goals.

First of all, we all have common goals, do we not? Perfection is everyone's common goal. Other than that we have other goals, spiritual and otherwise, that we set up for ourselves throughout experiences in the Universe. In generalities, no two goals are absolutely identical. It is as if we agree to go to a football game so we have the same destination. We get there and we sit side-by-side, but you cheer for Ohio State and I cheer for the University of Michigan. We had a common goal as far as location, but in the final analysis we differed. Common goals are the things that keep bringing people together, and it can bring them together throughout any number of lifetime experiences.

Similar Experiences

The other reason you might appear to be soul mates is that you have like experiences. After chasing around the Universe as many trillion-billion plus years that you have, and after taking as many spiritual steps up, down, and sideways as you have, and after leaving as many footprints and fingerprints behind you as you have, don't you think others have put a hand where you have put a hand or a footprint where you have stepped? Like experiences give you certain things in common, do they not? Sure, they do.

The fact is that you have put out so many of these soul impressions (these footprints) and other people have also put out soul impressions that are imposed upon another's impressions. They seem to fit one upon another. As a child you probably walked upon the sand or walked in the mud after a rain. Someone had previously walked along and left an imprint, and you put your foot into that imprint. You felt ten-feet-tall because your foot appeared to be as big as that one when it really wasn't. You simply stepped with an ability to have a similar match.

The experiences your soul has had are not unlike experiences that other souls have had. We now find two things that appear to bond two people together. When you join common goals and like experiences together into one condition, you find a tremendous bond between two people.

This is <u>not</u> at all a soul mate condition. Common goals and like experiences may parallel each other for a very long time. However, sooner or later the experiences will separate and go their separate ways. At some point, the patterns *may* crossover again and carry on.

Patterns are dependent upon the ability of the individual to absorb his or her experiences. Of course there is going to be a great feeling of friendship between two people when the patterns cross. There have also got to be separations. I truly don't think you would want to have it any other way. I don't think you would want to be attached to another soul because it does not give you the freedom of choice. You might say, "To be attached to another soul is not so much a detriment as it is an advantage. He is helpful to me, and I am helpful to him." If ever you are brought into proximity over and over again, or you do something with each other without freedom, you do not have control. You do not have the choices you want. It is just a matter of common goals and like-experiences that bring you together. It is not some kind of otherworldly destiny.

<u>Energy Impress</u>

This is a very important aspect that might be best-explained using graphics. Draw a circle. The circle represents the Universe. Put a line through the circle with the upper part representing the discarnate area of existence and the lower part representing the incarnate area of existence. Now draw lots and lots of little circles in the lower part of the large circle. Each of the small circles represents a soul, an individual in the incarnate area. Let us assume that we can isolate one circle that is you as an individual consciousness (a soul) under a microscope. After switching the dials, we can find that your consciousness has a certain level of understanding. We are

The Ubiquitous Soul   79

now going to assign a number to consciousness according to the level of spiritual understanding. After we have taken the totality of everything you have learned, and everything you are doing, and all the experiences your soul has been through, you have the ability to run the gamut of all levels. If we were to use the scale of one to ten and identify you as number seven, you can still run the gamut on levels one, two, three, four, five, six __, eight, nine, and ten.

Use the upper part of the large circle to represent the discarnate state in the Universe. We also have consciousness represented with billions and billions of little circles just as we have for where we are now in the incarnate state. Since a consciousness exists in the incarnate state and a consciousness exists in the discarnate state, we are going to remove just one consciousness and take a good look at it. Obviously, I am over-simplifying this in order to make a point.

When you are in the incarnate state vibrating, for example, as a seven and a consciousness in the discarnate state is vibrating as a seven, you have an absolute direct connection. The same thing is true when you are vibrating as a six and a consciousness in the discarnate state is vibrating as a six. You still have a connection. The point is simple. There is the ability of every individual to tap into a level of consciousness that is equal to that which is being used at that particular time. If you want some spiritual guidance, you put yourself at whatever level you wish, and you will be in contact with that level as it exists equal to yours in the discarnate state or anywhere else in the Universe. We are talking here about the whole Universe.

It is the Universe that has all of this wisdom and not soul consciousness, but consciousness comes into play because the Universe is all of these things. You have the ability to have all of the guidance, information, or whatever it is you want in a divine sense from any place in the Universe. What you do is attune your state of consciousness to any other state of consciousness. I used the number scale of one to ten to make the point, but you can use any scale you wish to make the point. You have the ability to tune into like frequencies.

My argument with the soul and over-soul theory is that advocates of that theory say that here you are, but the part of you that exists in the discarnate state is your guiding light that leads you along. <u>That is not true.</u> You cannot separate yourself from yourself any more than you can separate yourself, in all honesty, from the Universe or, if you prefer, the term 'God'. What <u>is</u> true is that there is action from what appears to be outside you that can be used and that can do you a great deal of good. It is not part of you separated and sitting up away from you. It is a part of consciousness that is another consciousness altogether, vibrating at the same frequency.

Energy is energy. As a soul (or, if you prefer, the word spirit), you are a point of energy. You are vibrating and that energy (like the energy of electricity) can be intensified or it can be lowered. Therefore, we can say the energy is at a certain level of intensity. Your intensity goes up as you raise your consciousness above the human and mundane level. You then become a more powerful energy, or what we call more spiritual at the soul energy level. The greater the energy output, the more spiritual you are. The lower the energy output, the less spiritual you are. As you go along, you can feel this in your body and in your mind as clarity or confusion. I am <u>not</u> talking about your intelligence level, nor am I talking about your experience level. I am talking about your state of consciousness, your energy level.

No two people have exactly the same rate. Because of the Law of the Universe, you (as 'A' for example) cannot superimpose your energy *exactly* upon an 'A' frequency in the discarnate. Let me put it this way: 'A' somewhere in the Universe can be in an energy state equal to you as 'A'. This allows you to move in and draw from 'A' whatever 'A' is capable of giving you. It is a Law of the Universe that whatever is known spiritually must be given upon demand. It is a spiritual sin to withhold that which you know. That would be a violation of the Law. Therefore, if you as an 'A' frequency tapped into an 'A' energy, and 'A' has an answer to your question, 'A' automatically <u>must</u> answer.

You can teach yourself to do this by teaching yourself to look for divine guidance. *God* cannot talk to you. *God* has no voice. *God* is an undefined, impersonal, divine, Intelligent energy. That is the energy you tie into.

<u>Illuminated</u>

There are all sorts of illumination. We can use the example of you as 'A' incarnate and the man we know as Jesus as 'A' discarnate. If you, as 'A' allow a certain amount of energy imposition upon 'A' which (for this example) is Jesus, then at that moment you are the recipient of all of his knowledge and all of his spiritual light. This can be a much illumined, mystical experience to you because it is so much greater than your level of knowledge at that time. This then becomes part of your knowledge experience.

There is great beauty and excitement in all of this. We have an enormous, infinite Universe filled with individual points of consciousness from which you can draw far beyond the level of experience and illumination that the so-called saints have. By keeping your horizons only close to what you know, you are denying yourself experiences far beyond your wildest dreams. In other words, you have got to reach. There *is* this tremendous knowledge that is transferred through soul energy that is indescribable. It is not accurate to explain this as a human sense experience.

Energy Points

Sometimes, *without knowing what you are doing*, you will raise yourself to an energy level and tap into another level. This is unfortunate to the extent it is unintentional because you are not prepared for it. Therefore, being unprepared, you lose much of the value. Teach yourself to realize there are all sorts of possibilities in this tremendous Universe. It is better for you to forget the idea of any over-soul that is wiser than you. No matter what knowledge you want, no matter what guidance you want, no matter what you seek, and no matter what the circumstances, there is a place in the Universe that can meet any one of your requirements. No matter *what*, somewhere, sometime, someone has had the experience and has the answer. Know there are other souls who have tread this pathway, also, and way beyond it. Know full well that you are on the pathway at your level of experience on earth. Know that you have come a long way and you have a long way to go. Know that you have got everything at your fingertips, but you have to be able to prepare yourself. You have to sit down and understand this is what you are dealing with, and that you are meant to have some concept of this *tremendous* Universe.

You have to lose the concept of people. You have got to give away the concept of someone talking to you as I am talking to you or seeing something with your human eyes. You have got to take on a whole _new_ concept of the something that is nothing, yet it is there. You have to look at the Universe as a vast nothingness filled with vast intelligent energy, and each one of those energy points are individualized; each one is a soul record of experiences.

All sorts of things can happen! You can contact that which you want. Better yet, through your desire and awareness of what you are dealing with, you can easily be put into any similar soul imprint you wish in order to garner the full intelligence of the experience. Jesus had certain experiences and certainly some great spiritual experiences. You can allow yourself to be put into his soul imprint.

I am going to use a negative example to make a point because the reaction to a negative experience can sometimes communicate more emphatically than a positive example. Have you ever been where there has been an accident or some kind of disaster, and did you not pick up quite a bit of the feeling of the experience of what happened just before you got there? To a certain degree, you have been set into the imprint that the other soul has made. To a certain extent, you have relived what that other soul has experienced. What you can now do is expand and imprint to the greater good.

You can put yourself into imprints all over the Universe. You can get all the sensations, all the feelings, all the knowledge, and everything you need. Don't sit there and say that it can't be done. It *can* be done. Eventually, it will be done. It has to be done because it is part of the experience at this particular point in space and time.

Singular Unity

Move yourself into the idea of unity in the Universe, thereby allowing yourself to become fluid to all the experiences of the Universe. At this point, experience abdicates the idea of individuality, singularity, and separation. This is a tricky point because it demands a lot of things. In the final analysis of our spiritual development on this plane, it demands your ability to reach out from this point and to be able to *feel* and to become part of the unity with the Universe without leaving this incarnated point. It can be done, but it is not an easy task, nor should it be. Among other things, it demands that you refuse to live on a separated, singular ego basis.

First of all, I am one. Since I am one, then God *and* I cannot exist. Then, since God exists, I do not. Therefore, since I do not exist, and only God exists, I am God and can experience God's Universe in totality. There you go. You spread yourself out and allow yourself to step into soul imprints all along the way. This is a great big Universe and not all of It is all that beautiful. By seeing the more mundane and rather ugly parts of the Universe, you have a greater appreciation for the beauty. In seeing all those things, you allow yourself to help others because the seeing in and of itself gives you the experience. How many of you feel it would be worth your experience to relive the experience of Jesus on the cross? If you venture to think about it, you would agree it would be worthwhile. Why? It would be worthwhile because you would be able to garner all of the intensity of man at his worst and man at his best. That is worthwhile intelligence and information!

There are certain experiences from which you can garner information without actually having the experience itself. When you superimpose yourself on the experience of an etheric consciousness, it is just a segment superimposition. You have not necessarily had the experience leading up to or following it. Nevertheless, you can draw from it that wonderful depth of truth. Many times this is extremely valuable, and you can say to yourself, "Ah, I don't have to walk that roadway. That I now know about. Therefore, I know how to circumvent that kind of pathway, and I also know what is necessary to bring me to a higher knowledge." Being responsible for your knowledge and vast experience <u>is</u> responsibility.

The Ubiquitous* Soul

Let me put it more simply. Here I have an eyedropper full of ocean water from the Pacific Ocean. I hold it up to indicate the ocean water in the eyedropper represents you. Then, I squeeze the drop of water back into the ocean. Where are you? Have you disappeared? No. If we had some means (and I had a way of doing it), we could get that exact eyedropper full of water back. It is now in the full ocean, but the drop of water is still a drop of water. It is everywhere at once. A portion of it is in the China Sea and another part of it may be up around Norway with yet another portion of it in Alaska. Who knows? It is wherever the current moves it. And if that water droplet was all intelligence, and the ocean was all intelligence, it would be everywhere. You are intelligence wherever you go with intelligence all around you. You are everything within everything. You are the ubiquitous soul.

You might say that the only experience you can have is the one as you sit where you are. Not so. When you sit there and think of your last vacation spot, you are actually at your vacation spot. When you are on a trip and picture your living room at home, you are actually in your living room, as well as, on your trip. In that same way (and for the same reason), you can be on Mars, Pluto, Venus, or anywhere else in the Universe you decide you want to go. It is a matter of saying to yourself, "I exist everywhere. I do not only exist

---

* Ubiquitous indicates being all places at one time.

here." Then, allow yourself to pull apart and become like a drop of water in the ocean. You are the ubiquitous soul.

In this idea of unity, where are you? You are nowhere and everywhere. Within the circle we have drawn, you do have your point of consciousness. However, within the larger circle we have drawn, there are no limits. There is no way of putting limits on you. You are every place at once. You are the ubiquitous soul.

In this huge, infinite, ever-expanding Universe
for which we have no definition, there are no limits.

Conclusion
To Earth from Second Earth

Part of growing is the experience as it unfolds.
--GT

Do not lose sight of the reality of our One, intertwined, single heartbeat. We do not breathe a breath that does not beat in your pulse. When you see a tree, we know the shade. Beneath the surface skin, muscles, bones, and hidden in valleys unexplored is the land we both come from and never left. You need not rediscover, for we are not a breath away. The valley of perfection and awareness takes us beyond love, beyond sensing, beyond anything you can hold, and anything we can show.

We know your vision could expand. You do not walk alone, struggle alone, or accomplish alone. Your life is our life. We have never left your side or you ours. There is never a time, a moment, a breath in the Universe in which we are separated. Your pain is our pain. Your joy is our joy.

We cannot shape your life. Be of strong faith. Be filled with belief in yourself that is unmatched, determined and brave. Most of all, be aware that every star, in every galaxy, in every course of the Universe can, if you will just turn, reflect your light. There is no end to that light. There is only an end to darkness.

Be of great peace for we love you dearly.

To Earth from Second Earth is a message delivered by Gregge Tiffen in the early 1970's

From The Collected Works of Gregge Tiffen

Life in the World Hereafter: The Journey Continues

Life in the World Hereafter Journal

First Encounter Series:
  No. 1 Into the Universe: Extraterrestrial Activities
  No. 2 Down to Earth: Terrestrial Activities
  No. 3 Earth and Second Earth

Questions and More Questions

2010 Booklet of the Month Series:
  The Journey Continues

2009 Booklet of the Month Series:
  The Language of a Mystic

2008 Booklet of the Month Series:
  Lessons in Living

2007 Booklet of the Month Series:
  Seasonal Reflections

2006 Thanksgiving: The Power of Prayer
2006 Winter Solstice: The Christmas Story

All publications are available
directly from P Systems
P.O. Box 12754
La Jolla, CA 92039

For Credit card orders and detailed descriptions visit:
www.P-SystemsInc.com/publications
For bulk orders call toll free: 1.888.658.0668

www.ingramcontent.com/pod-product-compliance
Lightning Source LLC
Chambersburg PA
CBHW071831290426
44109CB00017B/1799